WITHDRAWN

WITHDRAWN

INVISIBLE MAN
RACE AND IDENTITY

Twayne's Masterwork Studies
Robert Lecker, General Editor

INVISIBLE MAN
RACE AND IDENTITY

Kerry McSweeney

TWAYNE PUBLISHERS • BOSTON
A *Division of* G. K. Hall & Co.

Gramley Library
Salem College
Winston-Salem, NC 27108

Invisible Man: Race and Identity
Kerry McSweeney

Twayne's Masterwork Studies No. 17

Copyright 1988 by G.K. Hall & Co.
All rights reserved.
Published by Twayne Publishers
A Division of G.K. Hall & Co.
70 Lincoln Street
Boston, Massachusetts 02111

Copyediting supervised by Barbara Sutton
Book production by Gabrielle B. McDonald

Typeset in 10 pt. Sabon
by Compset, Inc., Beverly, Massachusetts

Printed on permanent/durable acid-free paper
and bound in the United States of America

Library of Congress Cataloging in Publication Data

McSweeney, Kerry, 1941–
    Invisible man.

    (Twayne's masterwork studies ; no. 17)
    Bibliography: p.
    Includes indexes.
    1. Ellison, Ralph. Invisible man.   2. Race awareness
in literature.   3. Identity (Psychology) in literature.
I. Title.   II. Series.
PS3555.L62515355   1988   813'.54   87-35838
ISBN 0-8057-7977-9 (alk. paper)
ISBN 0-8057-8027-0 (pbk : alk. paper)

for Mary Lynch

CONTENTS

NOTE ON REFERENCES
AND ACKNOWLEDGMENTS

Throughout this study I have referred to the title character and first-person narrator of *Invisible Man* as IM. I am not entirely happy about doing so, but consider it the least awkward way of dealing with the fact that this personage is never named in the text. I also pondered the question of whether Afro-Americans should be referred to as Negroes, the usual term at the time the novel was written, or as blacks, the more common contemporary designation. I have in the main chosen to respect the preference of Ralph Ellison. "I'm not black," Ellison has said. "I am a Negro-American writer. I emphasize Negro because it refers specifically to American cultural phenomena."

I am grateful to Robert Lecker for the opportunity to write about *Invisible Man* and to the following for their interest and assistance: David Williams, Robert Holton, Andrew Miller, Jim Critchley, Peter Sabor, Fanny Ellison, Lucy McSweeney, Susanne McSweeney, and the McGill University Humanities Research Grants Committee.

Quotations from *Invisible Man* are from the thirtieth-anniversary edition (New York: Random House, 1982).

The quotation on p. 27 from Louis Armstrong's recording of "Black and Blue" is used with permission: A. Razaf & R. Wally & H. Brooks, "Black and Blue" (What Did I Do To Be So), © 1929 (RENEWED 1957) by MILLS MUSIC, INC. International Copyright Secured   Made in USA   All Rights Reserved.

Ralph Ellison in 1952.

CHRONOLOGY: RALPH ELLISON'S LIFE AND WORKS

1914   Ralph Waldo Ellison born 1 March in Oklahoma City, Oklahoma, to Lewis Alfred Ellison, a former soldier, sometime candy-kitchen and restaurant operator, who had come to Oklahoma from Tennessee three years earlier as a construction foreman; and Ida Millsap Ellison, who had grown up on a farm in Georgia.

1917   Death of Lewis Ellison, who had become a small businessman selling ice and coal, leaves the family poor and forces Ida Ellison to find work as a domestic, custodian, and cook in order to support herself and her two sons.

1918   Taken with his younger brother, Herbert, to Abbeville, South Carolina, to visit grandfather Alfred Ellison, an illiterate ex-slave who had served as a local official during the Reconstruction before returning to driving a dray and chopping cotton while his wife worked as a washerwoman.

1931   Education in Oklahoma City's segregated school system ends with graduation from Douglass High School, where he had been first-chair trumpeter in the school band and its student conductor. During his high school years he also hears a number of well-known jazz musicians and sits in on rehearsals of the Blue Devils jazz band (forerunner of Count Basie's band).

1933   Leaves Oklahoma City by freight train to study music and music theory as a scholarship student at Tuskegee Institute in Alabama.

1935   Deeply engaged by T. S. Eliot's *The Waste Land*. "Eliot said
        something to my sensibilities that I couldn't find in Negro
        poets who wrote of experiences I myself had gone through."
        Begins seriously studying modern fiction and poetry, and be-
        gins writing his own poetry.

1936   Travels to New York to study sculpture and to find summer
        employment as a musician to pay for his last year at Tuskegee.
        Because of meager earnings decides to remain in New York;
        jobs during this period include server behind food bar at the
        Harlem YMCA, substitute receptionist and file clerk for psy-
        choanalyst Henry Stack Sullivan, and factory worker.

1937   Death of mother in Dayton, Ohio, in February. Spends winter
        there with his brother; they support themselves by hunting
        quail, which they sell to General Motors executives. "I had
        lived through my mother's death in that strange city, had sur-
        vived three months off the fields and woods by my gun. . . .
        Shall I say it was in those February snows that I first became
        a man?" In New York, meets Richard Wright through Langs-
        ton Hughes. With Wright's encouragement, composes his first
        book review and first short story.

1938   Friendship blossoms with Wright, who finds the young Ellison
        "terribly curious about art, the meaning of experience, and
        especially Negro experience." Employment with the New York
        City branch of the Federal Writers' Project, on which he works
        for nearly four years. Assignments include gathering material
        for a projected social history of the Negro in New York and,
        as part of the Living Lore Unit, studying the games and rhymes
        of Negro children and documenting other examples of urban
        and industrial folklore.

1938–1941   Contributes essays and reviews to the *New Masses* and other
        radical periodicals.

1939–1944   Eight short stories published. By 1940 no longer showing
        Wright "any of my writing, because by that time I understood
        that our sensibilities were quite different; and, what I was hop-
        ing to achieve in fiction was something quite different from
        what he wanted to achieve."

1942   Tries unsuccessfully to enlist in the Navy Band; becomes man-
        aging editor of the *Negro Quarterly*.

1943   Covers Harlem race riot for *New York Post*. "It was during
        the war and there was a lot of tension and after some alter-
        cation between a policeman and a Negro soldier and his
        mother and wife in a bar, Harlem just exploded and they

rioted for a day and a night and destroyed many of the white businesses. . . . Most of the business area in Harlem, the neighborhood grocers and so on, was shattered, looted, burned." Joins the merchant marine because he wants "to contribute to the war, but [not] be in a Jim Crow army"; serves for two years as sea cook.

1944   Awarded fellowship from the Rosenwald Foundation to write a novel. Affected by the experience of friends in the Army Air Corps, he plans a novel set in Nazi Germany in a prisoner-of-war camp, in which the ranking officer is a Negro pilot who has beneath him in rank a number of white pilots. "King of the Bingo Game" published in November; in this story he finds the "touch" he is searching for: "It had the realism that goes beyond and becomes surrealism."

1945   During summer, begins writing *Invisible Man* in a barn in Waitsfield, Vermont, while on sick leave from service in the merchant marine. "When I was struggling with a quite different narrative, it announced itself in what were to become the opening words of its prologue" ("I am an invisible man").

1946   Marries Fanny McConnell, his second wife, who helps support them during the seven years he works on *Invisible Man*. Other income comes from doing occasional writing and free-lance photography, building audio amplifiers, and installing high-fidelity sound systems.

1952   *Invisible Man* published in New York by Random House.

1953   *Invisible Man* wins the National Book Award and the National Newspaper Publishers' Russwurm Award.

1955–1957   In Rome as guest of the American Academy of Arts and Letters; begins work on a second novel.

1958–1961   Instructor in Russian and American literature at Bard College.

1962–1964   Teaches creative writing at Rutgers University.

1963   Huge second novel said to be almost ready for publication, a prediction intermittently repeated in following years. Eight excerpts from the work-in-progress published in periodicals between 1960 and 1977.

1964   Random House publishes *Shadow and Act,* a collection of essays, reviews, and interviews written over a twenty-two-year period and concerned with literature and folklore, Negro musical expression (especially jazz and the blues), and the relationship between the Negro-American subculture and North American culture as a whole. "Their basic significance . . . is autobiographical. . . . These essays represent . . . some of the necessary effort which a writer of my background must make in order to possess the meaning of his experience."

1965   In a *Book Week* poll, two hundred authors, editors, and critics select *Invisible Man* as the most distinguished novel published by an American during the previous twenty years. Refuses to attend a Negro writers conference held at the New School for Social Research, at which he is condemned by one participant for "standing outside of his people's struggle, making olympian remarks about how that struggle should be conducted."

1967   Substantial portion of the manuscript of second novel destroyed in fire that razes the Ellisons' summer home in the Berkshires.

1969   Well received during a March visit to West Point to speak to the plebe class; badly received by black students during April visit to Oberlin College to speak about the blending of American black culture and American white culture. Awarded the Medal of Freedom, America's highest civilian honor, by President Lyndon Johnson.

1970   Awarded the Chevalier de l'Ordre des Artes et Lettres by André Malraux, the French minister of cultural affairs.

1970–1980   Albert Schweitzer Professor of Humanities at New York University.

1975   Speaks at the opening of the Ralph Ellison Public Library in Oklahoma City.

1978   In a *Wilson Quarterly* poll of professors of American literature, *Invisible Man* is identified as the most important novel published in the United States since World War II.

1981   Tells interviewer that "if I'm going to be remembered as a novelist, I'd better produce a few more books."

1982   Random House publishes special thirtieth-anniversary edition of *Invisible Man*, with an introduction by the author.

1986   Random House publishes *Going to the Territory*, a second collection of essays, addresses, and reviews.

1

HISTORICAL CONTEXT

This is an era of hardboiled-dom. . . . Do you have feelings? There are correct and incorrect ways of indicating them. Do you have an inner life? It is nobody's business but your own. Do you have emotions? Strangle them. To a degree everyone obeys this code. And it does admit of a limited kind of candor, a closemouthed straightforwardness. But on the truest candor it has an inhibitory effect. Most serious matters are closed to the hardboiled. They are unpracticed in introspection. . . . If you have difficulties, grapple with them silently, goes one of their commandments. To hell with that! I intend to talk about mine.

Saul Bellow, *Dangling Man* (1944)

In the decade following the end of World War II, a number of important new American novelists emerged. There were large differences of regional origin, cultural background, and subject matter among them; but certain similarities were also recognizable. One of the most striking was the posture of revolt against the aesthetic and ethic of Hemingway, the most influential writer of the previous generation; and, at a more general level, against both Jamesian notions of the well-made novel and *Waste Land*–like expressions of spiritual exhaustion—both of which were perceived to have dominated the fiction of the previous decades. Saul Bellow threw down the gauntlet in the first paragraph of his first novel (quoted in epigraph), and two years later, in 1946, Ralph Ellison, a young American writer from a very different background, voiced an equally aggressive challenge in an essay called "Twentieth-Century Fiction and the Black Mask of Humanity." This essay sketched an argument that Ellison was to elaborate more fully in other essays, particularly in "Society, Morality, and the Novel" (1957). There he observed that the classic nineteenth-century American novelists—Hawthorne, Melville, Twain, and James—had all been "concerned with the moral predicament of the nation" and the values and cost of living in a democracy. By the 1920s, however, the writers had become distracted "from the realities of the moral situation." The novel form, "which in the hands of our greatest writers had been a superb moral instrument, became morally diffident and much of its energy was turned upon itself in the form of technical experimentation."

Ellison went on to argue that the ambitions of a contemporary novelist could be understood only in the light of the failure of the novelists of the 1920s, and he praised Bellow's sprawling picaresque novel of 1953, *The Adventures of Augie March,* in terms that he would unquestionably have been pleased to have applied to his own novel, *Invisible Man,* published in 1952: "It is characterized by a big conception of human possibility and a quality of wonder arising out of the mysteriousness of a reality which keeps its secret despite the documentation of the social scientists, and it is informed by a knowledge of chaos which would have left the novelists of the twenties discouraged. Certainly it confronts large areas of American reality which simply didn't get into the novels of the twenties." For Ellison, the task of the novelist was to achieve "for himself and for his readers some new insight into the human predicament, some new facet of human possibility." The novel was basically a form of communication; what was communicated was "a vision" of a particular experience that achieved "its universality, if at all, through accumulating images of reality and arranging them in patterns" of larger significance. If the novelist was successful, the "specific complex of experience" he dealt with would speak "metaphorically for the whole" and help to form its readers' "sense of humanity" and "conception of human value."[1]

The "specific complex of experience" that was Ellison's subject as a novelist was the life of Negro Americans. Deficiencies in the depiction of black characters by modern American novelists was the subject of "Twentieth-Century Fiction and the Black Mask of Humanity," written the year after Ellison began work on *Invisible Man*. Novelists, including Hemingway, Steinbeck, and the early Faulkner, seldom conceived "Negro characters possessing the full, complex ambiguity of the human." Rarely was an American Negro drawn "as that sensitively focused process of opposites, of good and evil, of instinct and intellect, of passion and spirituality, which great literary art has projected as the image of man." As Ellison pointed out in other places, the tendency to stereotype was hardly peculiar to novelists. A grotesque example was found in Park and Burgess's *Introduction to the Science of Sociology*, the standard textbook of its day, which Ellison had used at the Negro college he attended during the 1930s: "The Negro is, by natural disposition, neither an intellectual nor an idealist, like the Jew; nor a brooding introspective, like the East Indian; nor a pioneer and frontiersman, like the Anglo-Saxon. He is primarily an artist, loving life for its own sake. His métier is expression rather than action. He is, so to speak, the lady among the races."[2]

A central ambition of Ralph Ellison in *Invisible Man* was to depict the novel's central character and narrator as possessing "the full, complex ambiguity of the human." A precondition for the realization of this ambition and an equally central part of Ellison's creative intention was to depict something of the sweep and variety of what he calls the Negro-American experience. The black milieu so richly depicted in *Invisible Man* is not simply décor; it is the novel's macrosubject and the essential sociocultural context for the exploration of its moral and thematic interests. This is why the form of the book is episodic, allowing for the depiction of the varied character and varied types of black-American experience. In the same way, the essential historical context in which *Invisible Man* must be placed is the collective experience of black Americans from the Reconstruction period to World War II, "a scant eighty years," as Ellison described them in 1945, that "have sent the Negro people hurtling, without clearly defined trajectory, from slavery to emancipation, from log cabin to city tenement, from the white folks' fields and kitchens to factory assembly lines; and which, between two wars, have shattered the wholeness of its folk consciousness into a thousand writhing pieces."[3]

But one should rather say that the novel places itself in this larger historical context, for the events in the life of its nameless central character are designed to be representative of the experience of many black Americans during the twentieth century. The opening chapters epitomize the dynamics of black-white relationships in the prewar South, while the narrator's early ambitions recapitulate the strategy for Negro development propounded by Booker T. Washington, founder of the Tuskegee Institute in Alabama, which Ellison attended for three years and on which the college IM attends is clearly based. The narrator's passage from the South to New York City is representative of the large-scale migration during the early decades of the twentieth century in which the black American left behind "certain important supports to his personality": a relatively static social order that, while repressive, provided some sense of being "at home in the world"; a religion; a family structure; and a body of folklore that served "as a guide to action." To IM, as to the four hundred thousand Negro Americans who lived there, New York meant Harlem, the overcrowded and politically and economically exploited section of Manhattan that was "the scene and the symbol of the Negro's perpetual alienation in the land of his birth." For the narrator, as for many other northern blacks, Harlem meant the "desperate search for an identity."[4] As it does in the novel, this search led many to or toward industrial capitalism, the Communist party, and/or black nationalism (represented in the novel by the figure of Ras, which owes something to Marcus Garvey). The desperation could also lead to race riots (like one in 1943 that Ellison covered for the *New York Post* and on which chapter 25 of the novel is partially based). And for some it led to the psychiatric clinic in a brightly lit Harlem basement that Ellison described in "Harlem Is Nowhere," the 1948 essay from which I have been quoting. It is hard not to associate this room with the brightly lit basement room in which, in his novel's prologue, IM sits brooding and listening to Louis Armstrong sing, "What did I do to be so black and blue?"

The Afro-American context of *Invisible Man* also includes forms of artistic expression. For one thing, as a number of commentators have shown, Ellison's novel is part of a tradition of black prose narrative—autobiographies and fictional life histories—that includes the *Narrative of the Life of Frederick Douglass, an American Slave* (1845), Booker T. Washington's *Up from Slavery* (1901), James Weldon Johnson's *Autobiography of an Ex-Colored Man* (1912), Jean Toomer's *Cane* (1923), Zora Neale Hurston's *Their Eyes Were Watching God* (1937), Richard Wright's *Native Son* (1940) and *Black Boy: A Record of Childhood and Youth* (1945), James Baldwin's first novel, *Go Tell It on the Mountain* (1953), and more recent works such as the *The Autobiography of Malcolm X* (1965) and Claude Brown's *Manchild in the Promised Land* (1965).

Richard Wright's work has been thought to be of special importance to Ellison's literary development because of their close friendship during the first stages of Ellison's writing career. It is true that in a 1941 review Ellison praised *Native Son* highly ("the first philosophical novel by an American Negro . . . in the front rank of American fiction") and that four years later he was eloquent in his description of Wright's "most important achievement." "He has converted the American Negro impulse toward self-annihilation and 'going-underground' into a will to confront the world, to evaluate his experience honestly and throw his findings unashamedly into the guilty conscience of America."[5] And a number of critics have claimed that the prototype of the narrator's subterranean room in *Invisible Man* is found in Wright's overheated novella, *The Man Who Lived Underground.* Ellison has, however, consistently played down the notion that he was appreciably influenced by Wright. The big distinction to be made, according to Ellison, is between "relatives" and "ancestors": one can do nothing about choosing the former; but as an artist one can choose the latter. Wright and he were united by their "mutual interest in ideas and the craft of fiction"; but their sensibilities and backgrounds were different, and what the younger writer was trying to achieve in fiction was quite unlike Wright's mixture of naturalism, social determinism, and Marxist ideology, which prevented him from depicting in his fiction "a Negro as intelligent, as creative or as dedicated as himself."[6]

The forms of black American artistic expression that most influenced *Invisible Man* were folklore, jazz, and the blues, about each of which Ellison has had a good deal to say in interviews and in his critical prose, especially in the pieces collected in *Shadow and Act* (1964). For Ellison, folklore offered "the first drawings of any group's character" and was the record of its attempts "to humanize the world."

> It preserves mainly those situations which have repeated themselves again and again in the history of any given group. It describes those rites, manners, customs, and so forth, which insure the good life, or destroy it; and it describes those boundaries of feeling, thought and action which that particular group has found to be the limitation of the human condition. It projects this wisdom in symbols which express the group's will to survive; it embodies those values by which the group lives and dies.[7]

Folklore, then, was essential to the understanding and to the depiction of the informing spirit of black America. Moreover, a novelist who could learn to employ these motifs in his work could add richness to its texture and attain a degree of formal organization that increased the work's resonance. Folklore motifs, that is, could help channel "the deep personal necessity which cries full-throated in the work of art and which seeks transcendence in the form of ritual."[8]

Jazz was a different kind of formal influence on *Invisible Man.* Ellison's sense of this mode of creative expression was rooted in the example of the jazzmen he had known during his youth. Their "driving motivation" had been "the will to achieve the most eloquent expression of idea-emotions through mastery of their instruments. . . . The end of all this discipline and technical mastery was the desire to express an affirmative way of life through [a] musical tradition . . . that insisted that each artist achieve his creativity within its frame. He must learn the best of the past, and add to it his personal vision."[9] The influence of the blues was more direct and more pervasive. Not only are there blues singers within *Invisible Man* (including Jim Trueblood, Mary Rambo, and the cartman in chapter 9 who calls himself Peter Wheatstraw); the whole novel, which begins with its narrator listening to a blues song of Louis Armstrong, can be seen as "a blues odyssey" or rather as "the literary extension of the blues. It was as if Ellison had taken an everyday twelve-bar blues tune (by a man from down South sitting [underground] up North in New York singing and signifying about how he got there) and scored it for full orchestra."[10] As Ellison explained in an essay written the same year he began *Invisible Man:* "The blues is an impulse to keep the painful details and episodes of a brutal experience alive in one's aching consciousness, to finger its jagged grain, and to transcend it, not by the consolation of philosophy but by squeezing from it a near-tragic, near-comic lyricism. As a form, the blues is an autobiographical chronicle of personal catastrophe expressed lyrically."[11]

Important as folklore motifs, the jazzmen's example, and blues rhythms are to *Invisible Man*, these distinctive forms of black-American creative expression are not the predominant artistic influences on the novel. The informing artistic context is more literary and more richly varied. As Ellison has explained, what is "most important of all" in writing a novel, even more than "what you seek to depict," is perspective. "And the main perspective through which a writer looks at experience is that provided by literature—just as the perspective through which a physician looks at the human body is the discipline of medicine; an accumulation of techniques, insights, instruments, and processes which have been slowly developed over long periods of time."[12] One lens through which Ellison looked at his subject was

Dostoyevski's great novella *Notes from Underground* (1864), whose anonymous first-person narrator sits alone in his room brooding and thinking, tells the story of how he got to be where he is, and ends, like Ellison's protagonist, by suggesting that at some deep level he speaks for the reader. But more important than these resemblances, as Joseph Frank has observed, was "Ellison's profound grasp of the ideological inspiration of Dostoyevski's work, and his perception of its relevance to his own creative purposes—his perception, that is, of how he could use Dostoyevski's relation to the Russion culture of his time to express his own position as an American Negro writer in relation to the dominating white culture."[13]

T. S. Eliot and James Joyce are other ancestors. While at Tuskegee, Ellison had discovered Eliot's *Waste Land,* and had been impressed by its range of allusion and by the closeness to the jazz experience of the sensibility he found in the poem. (This discovery may be said to be indecorously commemorated in the overwritten passage near the beginning of chapter 2 of *Invisible Man* describing the broken fountain and empty cistern on the lawn of the college the narrator attends.) Like Eliot, Joyce helped to make Ellison aware of the playful possibilities of language, and no one who has read them both will doubt that the mixture of realistic and symbolic levels in *Ulysses,* as well as its stylistic and presentational variations, were a considerable influence on *Invisible Man.* André Malraux was another ancestor; his novels expressed a concern "with the individual caught up consciously in an historical situation" and provided nondeterministic insights "which allowed me to understand certain possibilities in the fictional material around me."[14] So was Hemingway; Ellison's strictures on Hemingway's limitations of vision and absorption in technique have to be supplemented by his acknowledgment of the elder writer's importance as "in many ways the true father-as-artist of so many of us who came to writing during the late thirties."[15]

We have already noted the importance of the principal nineteenth-century American novelists and their moral commitment to Ellison's conception of the novelist's task. To this should be added a word about the tradition of American humor, particularly the line that runs from southwestern humor through Mark Twain and on to William Faulkner and Erskine Caldwell, whose *Tobacco Road* made Ellison aware of the liberating potential of extravagant laughter. Such a perspective perhaps deserves more emphasis than it is often given by commentators, for *Invisible Man* not only makes use of comic motifs, it is also frequently a very funny book. Finally, there is the influence and example of William Faulkner, the greatest American novelist of the twentieth century, an influence by no means restricted to the all-hell-breaks-loose humor in *Invisible Man*. The most important point is that in his work Faulkner continued the moral tradition that was at the heart of the work of the nineteenth-century American novelists, and was himself an example of what the creative activity of the novelist could achieve. "He was born," Ellison has said, "with all the anti-Negro clichés of Deep South white society, but as he confronted his own work, he discovered the human reality that lay behind these stereotypes. In the end, he wrote more deeply about Negroes than most Negro writers. I'd like to achieve the same kind of freedom as a Negro writer and as a man."[16]

2

THE IMPORTANCE
OF THE WORK

The word [masterpiece] need not be pretentious. . . . Let us mean
by it a work of the literary imagination which is consistent, engaging, and dramatic, in exceptional degrees; which exhibits largely
mastered a human subject of the first importance; and which seems
in retrospect to illuminate the whole physical and spiritual situation
of which it was, by the strange parturition of art, an accidental
product. One easy test will be the rapidity with which, in the imagination of a good judge, other works of the period and kind will
faint away under any suggested comparison with it.

John Berryman, apropos *The Great Gatsby* (1946)

In the more than three decades since its first publication, the most
frequent and most influential commentator on *Invisible Man* has been
its author. In interviews, essays, and lectures, Ralph Ellison has explained his intentions and his methods, pointed out sources and influences, called attention to formal and structural devices, offered
interpretative comments on characters and incidents, and elucidated
his novel's themes. In sum, he has provided a substantial framework
within which to discuss his novel and assess its importance (a framework of which I have made use in the preceding chapter). For Ellison,

the principal gauge of the intrinsic importance of a novel is "the extent that it deals quite eloquently with its own material—that is, you move from the specific to the universal." He insists there is no reason why a novel "about a Negro background, about Negro characters, could not be effective as literature and in its effectiveness transcend its immediate background and speak eloquently for other people." The obligation of the novelist is "to try to write so truthfully and so well and eloquently about a specific background and about a specific form of humanity that it amplifies itself, becomes resonant and will speak to other people and speak *for* other people." The big questions for the American novelist, as Ellison eloquently phrased them in 1957, were these:

> How does one in the novel (the novel which is a work of art and not a disguised piece of sociology) persuade the American reader to identify that which is basic in man beyond all differences of class, race, wealth, or formal education? . . . How does one persuade readers with the least knowledge of literature to recognize the broader values implicit in their lives? How, in a word, do we affirm that which *is* stable in human life beyond and despite all processes of social change? How give the reader that which we do have in abundance, all the countless untold and wonderful variations on the themes of identity and freedom and necessity, love and death, and with all the mystery of personality undergoing its endless metamorphosis?[17]

There is nothing new about these criteria for assessing a novel, nor about Ellison's ambitions as a writer of prose fiction. Both are squarely in the great moralizing tradition of the realistic novel. Ellison's claims, for example, are essentially the same as those made by George Eliot in England in the middle of the nineteenth century when she spoke of "the greatest benefit we owe the artist [being] the extension of our sympathies. Appeals founded on generalizations and statistics [i.e., on sociology] require a sympathy ready made, a moral sentiment already in activity; but a picture of human life such as a great artist can give, surprises [readers] into that attention to what is

Gramley Library
Salem College
Winston-Salem, NC 27108

apart from themselves, which may be called the raw material of moral sentiment. [Art] is a mode of amplifying experience."[18] In realizing their intentions, both the author of *Invisible Man* and the author of *Middlemarch* use the same general strategy of blending their directly expressed thematic concerns and moral propositions with a densely textured, solidly specified, and vividly presented social world. Many are the variations played in *Invisible Man* on the themes of identity, freedom, and the mystery of personality; but they are no less central to the novel than is the manifold of wonderfully rendered aural and visual particulars: for example, the voices of Trueblood recalling his sweet nights in Mobile, Peter Wheatstraw singing about his woman, and Ras exhorting a mob; or the descriptions of the types who frequent the lobby of the Men's House, of the crowd at Tod Clifton's funeral, and of the clutter of household objects of the dispossessed couple, including the paragraph-long description of the spilled contents of a single drawer that the narrator picks up from the snow.

While the mixture of moral concern and felt life in *Invisible Man* is traditional, the formal means employed to shape and organize the material are modernist. In the artistic elaboration and presentation of its subjects, and in the degree of formal control employed, Ellison's novel has more in common with Joyce's *Ulysses* than with Eliot's *Middlemarch*. These elaborations include the patterns formed by recurring images, symbols, and motifs; the polyphonic organization of chapters, some of which have a realistic or narrative level, a representative sociohistorical level, and a symbolic level; the changes from chapter to chapter (and even within a single chapter) in style and presentational mode—from straightforwardly representational to expressionistic and surrealistic; and the intermittent use of techniques of defamiliarization (like the eruption of Jack's glass eye) and other devices that complicate the reader's engagement with the text. In my reading of the novel, close attention will be paid to the calculations and trade-offs involved in Ellison's employment of complex devices to turn the raw material of his subject matter into art. For the moment, one may say that one of the most striking and original features of *Invisible Man* is the counterpoint between a compelling story that is in its own right startlingly and sometimes horrifyingly eventful (there are no battle royals, police shootings, or race riots in *Ulysses*) and the high degree of artistic elaboration, which repeatedly invites the reader to reflect rather than to react.

While the guidelines supplied by Ellison for gauging the success of *Invisible Man* are unquestionably helpful, it is never a good idea to allow a creative artist to become, uncritically, a privileged commentator on his own work. "Never trust the artist. Trust the tale" was the famous advice of D. H. Lawrence in his book on classic nineteenth-century American literature.[19] It is equally prudent to keep this advice in mind in considering a novel that is widely regarded as a classic of twentieth-century American literature. For one thing, as we shall presently see, the most interesting critical discussion of *Invisible Man* to appear in recent years has persuasively pointed up a discontinuity between the reflexive artist within the novel and the reflective spokesman outside it. For another, it is hardly either self-evident or universally accepted that there is something "basic in man beyond all differences of class, race, wealth, or formal education" and something stable in human life beyond all processes of social change. Such claims will seem mystifying to some readers; and a careful reading of the text may well lead to the conclusion that the assertions of the teller are not substantiated in his tale.

Certainly some readers of *Invisible Man* have found it to be a much darker book than has Ellison in his *post factum* commentary; to have a centrifugal rather than a centripetal energy that moves in the direction of chaos and absurdity; and to be dominated by an imagination of disaster, in which the real is transmuted not into uplifting art but into nightmare. In literary-historical terms, this would mean that the importance of *Invisible Man* could be better focused by seeing it as an early postmodernist text rather than as a late flowering of the moral-realistic tradition. Certainly Philip Roth tended to see the novel this way in his 1960 survey, "Writing American Fiction," in which he spoke of the contrast between the programmatically upbeat tempo of much contemporary fiction ("Why is everybody so bouncy all of a sudden?") and his own sense of the stupefying, sickening, and infuriating quality of "much of American reality." As a counter to the empty affirmations of life he found in a number of contemporary novels, Roth placed

> the image of his hero that Ralph Ellison presents at the end of *Invisible Man*. For here too the hero is left with the simple stark fact of himself. He is as alone as a man can be. Not that he hasn't gone out into the world; he has gone out into it, and out into it, and out into it—but at the end he chooses to go underground, to live there and to wait. And it does not seem to him a cause for celebration either.[20]

The ending of *Invisible Man* will have to be examined later; it would be premature to assess Roth's description of it at this time. But one can note that as early as 1960 *Invisible Man* was regarded in a way that since then more and more readers and commentators have adopted: as a work that illuminates the physical and spiritual situation of which it was a product. In the late 1980s, it seems even less contentious to add that the novel exhibits largely mastered a human subject of the first importance; that it is consistent, engaging, and dramatic in exceptional degrees; and that only a very few novels of the past forty years do not tend to faint away in comparison with it.

3

CRITICAL RECEPTION

It is felt that there is something in the Negro experience that makes it not quite right for the novel. That's not true. It becomes important to the novelist because it is in this problem, as Faulkner makes us aware, that the American human conflict is at its most intense and dramatic. . . . That which for the sociologist presents itself as racial conflict becomes for the novelist the American form of the human drama.

Ralph Ellison, 1952 interview

The first published criticism of any novel comes in the form of reviews. Those of *Invisible Man* were copious and varied. At the egregious end of the spectrum was the review in the Communist *Daily Worker*, which assured the reader that "there are no real characters in *Invisible Man*, nor are there any realistic situations. The structure, the characters and the situations are contrived and resemble fever fantasy. . . . In effect, it is 439 pages of contempt for humanity, written in an affected, pretentious, and other worldly style to suit the king pins of world white supremacy." In the same vein was John Killens's review in the left-wing newspaper *Freedom*, which also used the criteria of socialist realism. "How," Killens inquires, does Ellison present the Negro people? The thousands of exploited farmers in the South are represented by a sharecropper who made both wife and daughter pregnant. The main character of the book is a young Uncle Tom who is obsessed with getting to the "top" by pleasing the Big, Rich White folks. A million Negro veterans who fought against fascism in World War II are rewarded with a maddening chapter [of] crazy Vets running hogwild in a down home tavern. The Negro ministry is depicted by an Ellison character who is a Harlem pastor and at the same time a pimp and numbers racketeer.

The Negro people need Ralph Ellison's *Invisible Man* like we need a hole in the head or a stab in the back.

It is a vicious distortion of Negro life.[21]

Few of the other reviews were as droll as the above, or anywhere as hostile. On the whole, *Invisible Man* was well received. Ellison was particularly fortunate to have his novel discussed in influential journals by five reviewers who were (or would become) distinguished writers or critics and who identified a number of the central points for critical consideration. In *Commentary,* Saul Bellow was lavish in his praise: "a book of the very first order, a superb book," which displayed "the very strongest sort of creative intelligence" in taking as its subject "this enormously complex and difficult experience of ours [for which] very few people are willing to make themselves morally or intellectually responsible." In the *American Mercury,* William Barrett described the novel as marking "a sensational entry by the Negro into high literature." There was social protest in the novel, but Ellison differed from Richard Wright in "grappling with the whole inner problem of the Negro as a human person, rather than as a mere social abstraction symbolizing an exploited class, and with a hero immensely more complex and intellectual" than Bigger Thomas, the central character of Wright's *Native Son.* Ellison had got hold of "a theme as big as America itself"—identity. He had recognized that it was perhaps the basic fact "of our national psychology that the American, in general, is not yet quite sure of his own identity." The novel was not faultless, however; as Barrett shrewdly observed, Ellison had been too sparing with his gift of characterization, and "in the struggle to make his story symbolic, rather than purely naturalistic, fiction, he has also made it somewhat abstract." This was especially true as soon as the narrator moved into the orbit of the Communist party. A nightmarish quality in the novel was also noted, or rather a combination of nightmare and realism that could only be compared to Céline's *Journey to the End of the Night,* a combination that accurately expressed the life of the Negro in America.[22]

In his review, Irving Howe did not fail to accentuate the positive. *Invisible Man* was "one of the most remarkable first novels we have had in years"; Ellison had an abundance of "primary talent," was "richly, wildly inventive" and had a magnificent ear for Negro speech. There were some serious shortcomings, however. One of them—this is an acute observation—was that Ellison had failed to establish an "ironic distance between the matured 'I' telling the story and the 'I' who is its victim. And because the experience is so apocalyptic and magnified, it absorbs and then dissolves the hero; every minor character comes through brilliantly, but the seeing 'I' is seldom seen." The middle section of the novel, concerning the Harlem Stalinists, also presented problems: it did not ring true, and its serious intention was undermined by its employment of caricature. Finally, Howe was bothered, as many subsequent readers have been, by the narrator's closing assertions of individuality and possibility; they seemed vapid and gratuitous, and it was telling that no attempt was made to specify the possibilities.[23]

For Richard Chase, writing in the *Kenyon Review,* the theme of *Invisible Man* was "the classic novelistic theme: the search of an innocent hero for knowledge of reality, self, and society." Chase was wary of the symbols with which the novel was "rather thickly endowed" and of "its tendency toward surrealism and jazz culture"; but he had to admit that the symbols were not asked "to carry more meaning than they can." (It did not occur to him to ask if they carried less meaning than they might have.) But the real weight of meaning in the novel was carried by "the profound underlying metaphor of 'invisibility,'" which not only contained social commentary but which had metaphysical, psychological, and moral dimensions. Finally, in the *Partisan Review,* Delmore Schwartz described *Invisible Man* as having so much actuality that it seemed irreverent to employ the language of literary criticism in speaking of it. He was given pause by the tendency "to melodrama, to declamation, to screaming, and to apocalyptic hallucination"; the novel was always "on the verge of going too far." But from this tendency, and from the status of being a protest novel, Ellison's book was redeemed throughout by its "persistent and generalizing insight into the hero's plight as a universal plight."[24]

This emphasis on the universality of the central character's predicament is an example of a marked tendency on the part of reviewers to regard *Invisible Man* as dealing with timeless difficulties that are everywhere and always the same, rather than with particular, historically and culturally conditioned problems rooted in the contradictions of a white capitalist society.[25] This same tendency can also be seen in a good deal of the academic criticism of *Invisible Man* published during the 1950s and 1960s—a tendency which, of course, was encouraged by Ellison's own commentary of his novel. One example was Robert Bone's survey, *The Negro Novel in America* (1958; revised 1965), in which *Invisible Man,* discussed in a section entitled "The Revolt against Protest: 1940–52," was flatly called "by far the best novel yet written by an American Negro." This judgment was hardly unconnected with Bone's belief that "art is a very different kind of human activity from politics" and that "to respect this distinction is the beginning of wisdom for the Negro novelist. The color line exists not between the covers of a book but outside, in the real world; its obliteration is a political, not a literary task."[26]

This kind of critical position began to take a lambasting in the later 1960s with the rise of black power, black aesthetics, and ideologically motivated criticism. So did the author of *Invisible Man,* who was perceived to be above the battle. In his *Black Aesthetic* (1972), for example, Addison Gayle, Jr., criticized Ellison for remaining "wedded to the concept of assimilation at a time when such a concept has ceased to be the preoccupation of the black writer." Four years later, in his introduction to *The Way of the New World: The Black Novel in America*, Gayle spoke wildly of "a new literary Renaissance" that had received its baptism of fire and blood in the riots of the mid- and late 1960s, and described the younger black novelist as a "machine gunner in the cause of mankind." Given such an excessively engagé critical position, it was perhaps surprising that Gayle's discussion of *Invisible Man* was not ungenerous and not impercipient. The slice-of-life aspect of the novel, for example, was highly praised; and the search for the novel's dominant theme was said to lead not only to the sources cited by Ellison—Dostoyevski, Melville and T. S. Eliot—but also to W. E. B. DuBois's *The Souls of Black Folk*. But for Gayle, *Invisible Man* had a central flaw—the character of the protagonist. This Achilles' heel was said to be attributable more to Ellison's political beliefs than to artistic deficiency; the invisible man "chooses death over life, opts for non-creativity in favor of creativity [*sic*], chooses the path of individualism instead of racial unity."[27]

A not dissimilar assault on Ellison was made by Irving Howe in his 1963 article "Black Boys and Native Sons," in which the promotion of Richard Wright's fiction ("The day *Native Son* appeared, American culture was changed forever") was accompanied by a corresponding demotion of Ellison and James Baldwin. It was a telling sign of the changes in critical climate that in the 1960s *Invisible Man* looked quite different to Howe than it had in 1952. What now struck him most about the novel was "the apparent freedom it displays from the ideological and emotional penalties suffered by Negroes in this country." Howe, a left-wing Jewish literary intellectual, insisted that "to write simply about 'Negro experience' with the aesthetic distance urged by the critics of the fifties, is a moral and psychological impossibility, for plight and protest are inseparable from that experience." If *Native Son* was marred "by the ideological delusions of the thirties," *Invisible Man* was marred (albeit "less grossly") by those of the fifties.[28]

Howe's attack prompted a strong and eloquent reply from Ellison in "The World and the Jug," which was reprinted in *Shadow and Act*. There were other ideological attacks on Ellison during the 1960s, some of them distinctly unpleasant—like his being called an Uncle Tom to his face by a black college student. In these episodes Ellison gave at least as good as he got, and usually better. His views on the role of the artist, the importance of form, and the inextricable linkage in American history and American life of white culture and black culture remained unchanged in the face of what he called "the straight-jacket of racist ideology."[29] The attacks did prompt Ellison to restatements and refinements of his views and seem to have led him to a deepened personal understanding of the connection between the creative process and the morality of fiction. As he told John Hersey in 1974:

> If the writer starts with anger, then if he is truly writing he imme-diately translates it through his craft into consciousness, and thus into understanding, into insight, perception. Perhaps, that's where the morality of fiction lies. You see a situation which outrages you, but as you write about the characters who embody that which out-rages, your sense of craft and the moral role of your craft demands that you depict those characters in the breadth of their humanity. You try to give them the density of the human rather than the nar-row intensity of the demonic. That means that you try to delineate them as men and women who possess feelings and ideals, no matter how much you reject their feelings and ideals. Anyway, I find this happening in my own work; it humanizes *me*. So the main motive is not to express raw anger, but to present—as sentimental as it might sound—the wonder of life, in the fullness of which all these outrageous things occur.[30]

All things considered, it is very hard not to feel that in his quarrel with militant blacks Ellison had the last and best word when he observed in 1977 that "the only way to win a fight with a book is to write a better book."[31] Certainly there has been a growing critical consensus over the past two decades that no better work of American fiction than *Invisible Man* has been written since the end of World

War II. This consensus has grown in tandem with the stream of academic criticism of the novel. A certain amount of this by now considerable body of secondary material has been useful in elucidating one or another of the rich variety of strands in the novel's fabric. Readers like myself who are at a distance from black American culture will have been particularly grateful for the work that has been done on the folklore and blues motifs in the novel and on its place in the Afro-American literary tradition. It is fair to say, however, that very little of the academic critical discourse on *Invisible Man* is indispensable and that the great majority is canonical, in that it implicitly or explicitly examines the novel within the frameworks provided by Ellison. Indeed, one critic has even spoken of there being "almost a mathematical consistency between Ellison's critical pronouncements and his creative performance."[32] It follows that most of this critical discourse is constructive, at least implicitly idealizing, and illustrative of the accuracy of John Bayley's observation that "the usual criticial instinct is to show that the work under discussion is as coherent, as aware, as totally organized as the critic desires his own representation of it to be."[33]

Two exceptions to these generalizations have appeared in the *Publications of the Modern Language Association (PMLA)*. In his "To Move without Moving: An Analysis of Creativity and Commerce in Ralph Ellison's Trueblood Episode," Houston A. Baker, Jr., drew upon poststructuralist theory and Marxist criticism in his analysis of the "brilliant reflexivity" of chapter 2 of *Invisible Man*. A teller of tales like his creator, Trueblood is both merchant and creative genius. Black folk-expression was "a product of the impoverishment of blacks in America," and "to make their products commensurate with a capitalistic marketplace, folk artists may even have to don masks that distort their genuine selves. Ralph Ellison is a master of such strategies." But one could find authorial self-awareness of this mastery only in the practice of "the *reflexive* artist" and "creative genius," not in the critical practice of "the *reflective* spokesman" and "merchant."[34]

In her "Ritual and Rationalization: Black Folklore in the Works of Ralph Ellison," Susan L. Blake brought a sophisticated understanding of folk expression, myth, and ritual to bear on the texts of Ellison's creative works. Like Baker, she called attention to a split between Ellison the critic and Ellison the creative artist. In his commentary on the battle-royal episode of his novel, for example, Ellison emphasized its symbolic and mythic elements; this led him to "ignore, minimize, distort, or deny" the peculiarities of black-American folk expression and the social conflict at its heart. Thus, the social meaning of the battle royal was contradicted and negated; a social experience was transformed into a mythic one. Furthermore, when *Invisible Man* was closely examined, Blake found that while the novel "presents itself as an epic statement of the need for black self-definition," the definition that the novel attributes to the folk tradition turns out to be the very one maintained by the whites. "Thus the result of the protagonist's identity quest is not self-definition at all but reaffirmation of the identity provided by the white culture."[35]

Something of the freshness of Baker's and Blake's analyses and of the way they stand out from the mass of critical commentary on *Invisible Man* can be indicated by recalling G. K. Chesterton's observation, "Either criticism is no good at all (a very defensible position) or else criticism means saying about an author the very things that would have made him jump out of his boots."[36] I do not imagine that anything in the following pages will leave the author of *Invisible Man* in his stocking feet. On the other hand, I do not intend to offer a canonical reading of the novel. In the end, as A. C. Bradley long ago remarked, a critic can only offer to others his own considered experience. What I offer is a reading of *Invisible Man* informed by my experience as a reader of prose fiction and as a longtime admirer of Ellison's novel. The personal experience I bring to the text is not that of an Afro-American but of an Irish-American whose firsthand experience of Harlem has been restricted to what was seen from the windows of Croton-line commuter trains during childhood and adolescence. I am, however, one of the "you" whom the narrator of *Invisible Man* addresses in the closing words of the novel, and for whom he suggests he may be speaking. Much of my reading will be concerned precisely with the subject of the relationship between the narrator and the reader, and with what Ellison has called the "most necessary" collaboration of the reader "in bringing the fiction into life," which presupposes not only "a body of shared assumptions" but also the "acceptance of a set of artistic conventions."[37]

A READING

4

PROLOGUE AND CHAPTER 1

How will it end
Aint got a friend
My only sin
Is in my skin
What did I do
To be so black and blue?
Louis Armstrong recording of "Black and Blue"

Invisible Man employs one of the staple conventions of prose fiction, a retrospective first-person narrator—the same narratorial device used in such central American novels as Hawthorne's *Blithedale Romance*, Melville's *Moby-Dick*, Fitzgerald's *Great Gatsby*, and Salinger's *Catcher in the Rye*. In novels so narrated there is a distinction to be made between the "I" as character and the "I" as narrator—between the younger, experiencing self who participates in and/or observes the events recounted in the narrative and the older narrating self who does the telling. In some novels, for example *The Catcher in the Rye*, where the temporal distance between the experiencing self and the narrating self is only a year, the distinction is relatively unimportant. But in other novels—*The Blithedale Romance* and *Moby-Dick* are examples—it is crucial for the reader to distinguish between the "I" as character and the "I" as narrator and not allow the two to become conflated.

On first reading, there would seem to be no difficulty for the reader of *Invisible Man* in distinguishing IM the character from IM the narrator and no particular reason to be alert to do so. The narrating self addresses the reader directly in present narrative time in the prologue and epilogue. He explains in the former that he feels a "compulsion to put [his] invisibility down in black and white"; he will tell the story of his earlier life for both expressive and communicative reasons, both to discharge emotion and to enable the reader to understand how he came to be in his present state—living underground in hibernation, "snarled in the incompatible notions that buzz within my brain." The twenty-five chapters in between the prologue and epilogue clearly pertain to IM the character. In them, the narrating self recounts the events from the time of his graduation from high school to the point at which he began to live underground—a crucial period of development that encompasses his rite of passage from adolescence to the threshold of maturity. It would seem patent that in these chapters the narrating "I" is content to restrict the point of view to that of his younger self, the experiencing "I", and to report and re-create with minimal retrospective interpolation what his younger self thought and did in the past. There are some exceptions to this generalization, of course, but they might be thought so clear-cut and so few in number as simply to prove the rule. At the beginning of chapter 2, for example, when the statue of the college founder removing the veil from the eyes of a kneeling slave is described, there can be no doubt that it is the narrator, seeing the scene "in my mind's eye," who is "unable to decide whether the veil is really being lifted, or lowered more firmly in place." Such reflections could hardly be those of IM the character, who at this point in his story is wholly cocooned in the mystifications of the college. For the same reason, in chapter 5, it is clearly the narrating self who describes the stage of the college chapel as the place where "the black rite of Horatio Alger was performed to God's own acting script."

Prologue and Chapter 1

But if *Invisible Man* is reread more reflectively and critically than the narrative pull of the text encourages one to do on first reading, one begins to see that the distinction between experiencing self and narrating self is more complex and problematic than it may have initially appeared. Take, for example, the opening paragraph of chapter 5, which describes what IM sees as he and his fellow students at the college walk through the growing dusk to the chapel. Unlike the descriptions of the campus in earlier chapters, this paragraph is written with an expressive intensity that reaches its crescendo with the description of a minatory blood-red moon looming behind the chapel like "a white man's bloodshot eye." It is not easy to decide whether the expressive distortion here registers the ominous mood and tense forebodings of IM the undergraduate or whether IM the narrator is deliberately using a distorting lens in order to project onto the scene his retrospective understanding of the underlying meanings of the situation.

A different example of the same difficulty is found in chapter 25 when IM, having fallen into a manhole while running from two white youths armed with baseball bats, replies to the taunts of his pursuers by suddenly laughing and saying, "But I still have you in this brief case"—the prize briefcase that contains his personal documents. What does IM the character mean by this cryptic statement? When asked the question at West Point in 1969 Ralph Ellison took authorial responsibility for the statement and explained that "what I wanted him to be saying" was that the white men "were not aware that *their* fate was in this bag that he carried—this bag that he had hauled around with his various identifications, his diploma, with Clifton's doll, with Tarp's slavery chainlink, and so on; that this contained a very important part of their history and of their lives."[38] I would myself prefer to assign the responsibility for IM's remark to the retrospective narrator within the text of *Invisible Man*, rather than to the author outside the work. But in either case, the result is the same: a fissure in the realistic surface of the text caused by making IM the character the mouthpiece for an after-the-fact generalization that it is wholly implausible to assign him (the character) *in propria persona*.

One could argue that these examples are simply two more insignificant exceptions to the rule, and that while they may be infelicitous, they hardly make for any serious reading complications. But it is better to say that these examples remind us that there is available to IM the narrator more than one mode through which to represent the key events in his earlier life, and that the straightforwardly reportorial-realistic (as it might be called) is only one such mode. In fact, a principal function of both the prologue and chapter 1 of *Invisible Man* is precisely to make the reader aware of this—to sensitize him to non-representational effects and alert him to the terms of the fictional contract he will be entering into if he continues to read.

Ralph Ellison has said that the prologue to his novel "was written afterwards. . . . I wanted to throw the reader off balance—make him accept certain non-naturalistic effects. It was really a memoir written underground, and I wanted a foreshadowing through which I hoped the reader would view the actions which took place in the main body of the book."[39] The principal foreshadowings in the prologue that help focus the reader's subsequent perception of the text are thematic: the leitmotivs of invisibility, sight and insight, identity, alienation, freedom, boomeranging, and the spiral of history are all first sounded in the novel's overture.

Other recurrent elements also make their first appearance in the prologue. One of them is the use of background music, a salient feature of the novel that is often overlooked. More than any other contemporary American novel one can think of, *Invisible Man* has the wherewithal to be the basis for a magnificent motion picture; it is a sorry comment on the state of the American film industry that the most distinguished novel of the past forty years has never been filmed. If it ever is adapted for the screen, it will be found to be already supplied with a sound track. In chapter 9, a man on a bus is overheard whistling the lugubrious jazz tune "They Picked Poor Robin," which ironically comments on the state of IM, who has just realized he has been cruelly duped. At the beginning of the factory hospital chapter, in which IM finds himself a pawn in the hands of high-powered medical technocrats, the opening bars of Beethoven's Fifth Symphony keep running through his head. "Jelly, Jelly / Jelly, / All night long" blares from a juke box in a Harlem bar while dancers moil in the smoke-green haze; and in a Spanish bar in another chapter, the juke box plays "Media Luz." More important, a number of black spirituals and folk songs are heard during the novel, including two moving expressions of "the old longing, resigned, transcendent emotion" (chap. 21) that was a traditional response of black Americans to their plight. "Lead me to a rock that is higher than I" is sung during the chapel scene, and "There's Many a Thousand Gone" at Tod Clifton's funeral.

The blues, another distinctively Afro-American response to the same plight, is the dominant musical form on the novel's sound track, and the most tellingly deployed. In the prologue, IM sits brooding as he listens to recordings of Louis Armstrong playing and singing "Black and Blue," the first of several blues songs heard in the novel. In chapter 6, as he walks across the college campus just after learning of his expulsion, the sound of an "old guitar-blues plunked from an out-of-tune piano" drifts toward IM, reminding him of the echoed whistle of a lonely train. Three chapters later, now in New York, IM encounters a cartman belting out the "Boogie Woogie Blues." As he goes on his way a few pages later, the volume of his singing diminishes and IM is again reminded of "the sound of a railroad train highballing it, lonely across the lonely night." Later, Mary Rambo is overheard singing a Bessie Smith song, the "Backwater Blues"; a record shop loudspeaker blares out a languid blues as IM walks along 125th Street; and finally, in the epilogue, on the novel's very last page, IM recalls Louis Armstrong playing and singing "Buddy Bolden's Blues."

But the first and most important point Ellison made in commenting on what he was up to in the prologue was that he wanted to throw the reader off-balance and prepare him to accept certain nonnaturalistic effects. One result of doing so is to enable the reader to experience an aesthetic equivalent of the sharpened and sensitized perceptions that the narrator's acceptance of his invisibility has given him. It has, he says in the prologue, made him have "a slightly different sense of time, [because] you're never quite on the beat. Sometimes you're ahead and sometimes behind. Instead of the swift and imperceptible flowing of time, you are aware of its nodes, those points when time stands still or from which it leaps ahead." The principal way in which the reader is sensitized to this is through the reefer-induced vision at the center of the prologue. The spell of the reefer draws IM into a shifting dreamworld containing several richly suggestive images of America's racial past. The tableau of the ivory-colored girl with a voice like his mother's, pleading before slave owners, gives way to the voice of a backwoods black preacher whose text is the "Blackness of Blackness," a color that is said to both make you and unmake you. His rant is then replaced by the voice of an old singer of spirituals. She raises in a different way the subject of black-white sexuality, and exemplifies the intense ambivalence of black emotions toward whites, when she says that she dearly loved her master and the sons he gave her even though she hated him too. But something she loved even more was freedom, which did not lie in hating. When asked what this freedom is that she loved so well she gives an answer that the reader of *Invisible Man* would do very well to remember when he comes to the novel's epilogue. "I guess now it ain't nothing but knowing how to say what I got up in my head. But it's a hard job, son. Too much is done happen to me in too short a time." And just before the dream vision ends we hear IM call out to two persons named Ras and Rinehart, who much later in the novel will be discovered to be exemplary figures in the American racial present.

The spell of the reefer is the first of a number of nonnaturalistic dreamlike nodes that are effectively deployed in *Invisible Man*. These moments of heightened symbolic and expressive suggestiveness include IM's dream of going to the circus with his grandfather at the end of chapter 1, Trueblood's dream in chapter 2, the hallucinatory-like experience of IM in the factory hospital in chapter 11, and the castration dream at the end of chapter 25. There are, in addition, other episodes in the novel that seem dreamlike to a greater or lesser degree and that, at the least, may be described as being not quite on the beat of realistic narrative. The scene with Brockway in the paint factory basement is an example ("as in a dream . . . things were speeding up"); another is the series of significant events that occurs in chapter 13 ("there was a quality of unreality over the whole afternoon"); and the "awake or dreaming" (IM is not sure which) experience in chapter 19, in which the early-returning husband of the white woman who has seduced IM looks into his wife's bedroom to say hello but doesn't seem able to see the black man next to whom she is sleeping.

The distorting nodes and nonnaturalistic effects in *Invisible Man*, however, are not only found in the dream scenes; they are also embedded in the particulars of the realistic narrative. Consider, for example, IM's claim in the prologue that in his battle with Monopolated Light & Power he has fought back by wiring his basement room so that it now has exactly 1,369 lights. Is this to be believed? Wouldn't the heat of so many lights in one room melt the vanilla ice-cream covered with sloe gin, which is his favorite dessert? Isn't IM being extravagantly hyperbolic, even to the point of mendacity? And didn't Ralph Ellison, in one of his many after-the-fact comments on *Invisible Man*, call IM "something of a liar, if you ask me"?[40] On the other hand, the circumstantial detail—the exact number of the lights, which are not "fluorescent bulbs, but . . . the older, more-expensive-to-operate type, the filament type"—does suggest that one is being told the literal truth. While it is difficult for the reader to know what to think of this particular question, the larger and more important point should be clear. Even if IM's claim about the number of lights in his room is not exaggerated, the gesture of so wiring his room is not only exaggerated but extravagantly, even obsessively, expressive of his estrangement from the world outside his basement room. As one finishes the prologue and begins to read his retrospective account of how he got to be where he is, one might well wonder whether, in the narrative IM is composing in his too-well-lit underground room, there will be found similar exaggerations and extravagances that will strain credulity, distort the realistic surface, and possibly break the representational illusion.

This in fact turns out to be the case. There are a number of such off-the-beat nodes in the narrative of *Invisible Man,* and since they have puzzled and/or bothered many readers of the novel, we had better reflect on them here. Let us first consider the question of symbols, of which bold, sometimes flagrant use is made. A rough-and-ready description of symbol would be a physical object that, through conceptual transference, comes to represent or stand for some nonphysical value, state, or idea. In considering this question, it is important to notice who is making the transference. In *Invisible Man* a number of objects are given symbolic status by a character within the novel, not by the narrator (or the implied author). "I yam what I am," exclaims IM the character in chapter 13, in a spirited adaptation of the Lord's statement to Moses in Exod. 3:14. What IM has done is to make the hot buttered yam he is eating on a snow-covered Harlem street into an emblem of his cultural roots in the South, which he had been denying. In reaffirming these roots he uses the yam as a synecdochical symbol of a psychological complex of memories, pieties, and tastes. Similarly, when Tarp says in chapter 18 that the piece of filed steel he is giving IM has "a heap of signifying wrapped up in it," he means, first of all, that this physical reminder of his years on a chain gang means a lot to him and that, at a more general level, it is a reminder of the oppression of the Negro in America. When Tarp gives the link to IM, the rising black leader, he is performing a symbolic act of the passing-the-torch variety.

But there are other symbols, or symbol-like effects, in *Invisible Man* that cannot be ascribed to a character within the novel. They are narratorial or authorial symbols (I shall consider them as the former). The examples that draw the most attention to themselves are those that are baldly symbolic—highfalutin, stagy signifying that seems out of place in a novel that devotes so much of its energy and attention to the realistic depiction of its world. Two notorious examples are the revelation at the end of chapter 6 that the Reverend Homer A. Barbee, who falls flat on his face on the chapel platform after finishing his speech, an epic mythologizing of the life of the college founder, is as blind as his namesake, the Greek epic poet; and the eruption of Jack's previously unmentioned glass eye onto the table during a heated exchange at the Brotherhood meeting in chapter 22—an ocular pratfall that seems no less gratuitous than Barbee's fall and that has left some readers with the same feeling that IM has as he leaves the meeting: "I felt as though I'd been watching a bad comedy."

Of course it is possible to talk interpretatively about these two symbolic incidents and to relate them to central thematic motifs in the novel having to do with sight and insight, seeing and not seeing. In fact, it is not only possible but all too easy to do so. But doing so does not really answer the question of why redundant and unsubtle effects like these are included in such a carefully articulated and highly polished text. After all, it is hardly the case that the narrator of *Invisible Man* is incapable of a much more nuanced and suggestive use of symbolic effects. Probably the best way to think about the revelations of Barbee's blindness and Jack's half-blindness is not in terms of their meaning but of their effect on the reader's experience of the novel. They are bound to affect the verisimilar illusion, to encourage a more thoughtful and critical reading, and to remind one that the artistic organization of the novel is as important to the reading experience as the story line and that there are expressive, as well as communicative, urgencies shaping this first-person narrative.

Some other symbolic motifs or episodes in *Invisible Man* are less gratuitous but are nonetheless imperfectly integrated into the realistic surface. At least for readers like myself, who are as interested in the world of the novel as in the work of art, they can be just as bothersome as Jack's glass eye. Take, for example, the moment at the end of chapter 20 when the narrator follows into a subway car the three young men he has been thinking about. There he sees standing across from each other a white nun dressed in black and a black nun dressed in white, each looking at the other's crucifix, a sight which conveniently supplies fresh material for meditation. It is hard not to regard this little symbolic tableau as excessive. Of course it is true that one is liable to see almost anything in the New York City subway, and it could be argued that if during an earlier subway ride at the end of chapter 11 IM could see a young platinum blonde nibbling a red Delicious apple, why in chapter 20 shouldn't he be allowed to see two nuns belonging to different religious orders in the same car? And citing the work rather than the world, one could also argue that the appearance of the black and white nuns is artistically prepared for by the patterning of black and white that runs through the novel.

The problem, as I see it, is not one of kind, but of degree. The black and white nuns are too overtly deployed. It would have been better if they were more in the background, more peripheral, and if the narrator had, so to speak, seen them out of the corner of his eye or—to change from a visual to an aural image—if this symbolic pairing had *pinged* on the reader's awareness rather than *banged* on it. After all, as one knows from a number of places in the text, the narrator of *Invisible Man* is capable of subtle and suggestive symbolic effects that resonate rather than dully thud; that tease the reader into further thought and a deeper engagement with the text; and that are at the same time fully integrated into the realistic narrative. As we shall see, the premier example in *Invisible Man* is the superlative scene in the paint factory in which IM is told to mix ten drops of black paint into buckets of white paint. And there are other scenes where there is a satisfying (if less impressive because more delimited in meaning) fit between the realistic and the symbolic levels: IM's unsuccessful attempts in chapter 15 to get rid of the broken cast-iron figure of the wide-mouthed grinning Negro; and the burning of the contents of his briefcase in chapter 25.

The fact nevertheless remains that the narrator of *Invisible Man* sometimes chooses to be splashy and overt in his deployment of symbols—sometimes even pointlessly so, as in chapter 2 when, as he listens to Jim Trueblood tell the story of his coupling with his daughter, the character IM is made to pick up from the porch and gaze at "a hard red apple stamped out of tin," which doubtless reminds him, as it of course does the reader, of the crisis point in the Garden of Eden. The major danger in the narrator's spicing his narrative in this way is that it sets up certain reader expectations. Pascal said that there were two errors: to take everything literally and to take everything spiritually (i.e., symbolically). In the case of *Invisible Man,* the more likely error is that the reader will be led to take everything symbolically. It is a peril to which even excellent commentators on the novel have succumbed. Consider that favorite dessert of vanilla ice cream and sloe gin mentioned in the prologue. Marcus Klein explains it as "white, presumably, seeping blood," while Robert O'Meally sees a "mock patriotic" motif of red, white, and blue (the last color supplied by the Louis Armstrong record).[41] Can't a man, even one living underground, indulge a sweet tooth and do so with something more pleasing to his taste than, for example, the cheesecake offered him by Jack in the cafeteria scene in chapter 13, a dessert that the yam-eating young Negro from the South had never tasted?

In reading *Invisible Man,* then, the extreme of taking everything symbolically should be avoided. But what about the other extreme—taking everything literally? This is a serious potential danger, one that requires sophistication and tact on the part of readers of realistic novels, especially novels like *Invisible Man* that present their material with a high degree of artistic elaboration. To put the question bluntly: To what extent does it make a difference to the reader's experience of *Invisible Man* whether or not there is a factual basis to the scenes and incidents described?

In chapter 3, for example, which is set in the Golden Day bar/brothel, we have broad comedy and zany goings-on plus a Freudian overlay. But the condition of the vets—dispossessed members of the Negro middle class who have become psychologically unhinged because of the contradictions in American society—is anything but droll. Is the chapter rooted in the all-hell-breaks-loose traditions of southwestern humor, or in sociological reality? How can one tell? Does it help to know that Tuskegee, Alabama, the home of the Tuskegee Institute founded by Booker T. Washington, which Ralph Ellison attended and on which the college in his novel is obviously modeled, was also the site of a United States Veterans Administration Hospital for Negroes? In chapter 11, does it make any difference whether physicians in New York–area hospitals really did use electric shock therapy on black victims of industrial accidents and whether they chose this procedure from a range of possible treatments that included prefrontal lobotomy? Does the account of the race riot in chapter 25 become a more gripping piece of writing once one knows that there have been serious race riots in Harlem and that the one in 1943 was covered by Ralph Ellison for the *New York Post?* Conversely, does the chapter gain or lose in intensity of reader engagement if one gives priority to artistic considerations—as Ellison himself did when he described the chapter as "an imaginative construction which is based upon pattern" (albeit with "reality behind it")?[42]

The short form of the answer to such questions must ultimately be that good novels are self-authenticating and must be allowed to conduct themselves on their own terms. The terms that *Invisible Man* implicitly proposes in its prologue and opening chapters are that the novel will offer a basically realistic narrative, but one with expressive, sometimes expressionistic, distortions, nonnaturalistic effects, and a high degree of artistic elaboration. It is further implied that the novel will require the reader to be aware of the nodes in the flowing of time and to be attuned to changes in mood and tempo that include the fast forward of the opening pages of chapter 5 and the slow motion of the description of Tod Clifton's shooting in chapter 20. Even the character IM is aware of the great differences that a change in the beat can cause: as he reflects in chapter 10, if one "could slow down his heartbeats and memory to the tempo of the black drops falling so slowly into the bucket yet reacting so swiftly, it would seem like a sequence in a feverish dream." It is in more or less this same slow tempo that a number of movements in *Invisible Man* are played. In chapter 25, for example, running "as in a dream," IM encounters Ras, "the Destroyer," "upon a great black horse" looking like a figure from the Apocalypse (his appearance has been preceded by the sound of "a precise and hallucinated" voice crying about the drawing nigh of the coming of the Lord). But Ras appears this way only to the exacerbated consciousness of IM. To the two blacks calmly drinking from a bottle, whom IM overhears a short while later, Ras is a figure of fun—a splendidly comic sight "riding up and down on this ole hoss, you know, one of the kind that pulls vegetable wagons . . . that crazy sonofabitch up there on that hoss looking like death eating a sandwich."

We can attempt a longer, though less direct, answer to the question of the relationship of literal to symbolic or figurative in *Invisible Man* (and of the relationship of factual basis to quality of reader engagement) if we consider chapter 1, in which the terms of the fictional contract are still being presented. The chapter describes what is perhaps the most appalling example in the entire novel of the whites' treatment of blacks: the battle royal staged in the ballroom of the main hotel of a southern town as part of the evening's entertainment for its leading white male citizens—"bankers, lawyers, judges, doctors, fire chiefs, teachers, merchants." Ten Negro boys are provided with boxing gloves, put in a makeshift ring, and blindfolded. They then fight each other for the amusement of the audience, which has already grossly enjoyed both the dancing of a naked blonde and the discomfiture of the black youths forced to watch her. The boxing concludes with IM slugging it out with the biggest of the boys until he is pounded to the canvas. Then the sweat-drenched boys are shown a rug covered with coins and a few bills and told to go and get their money. When they do so the current in the electrified carpet is turned on. Finally, IM is invited to deliver his graduation speech on the theme of social responsibility, which he does while swallowing blood until he is nauseated. His audience, however, pays no attention to his sonorous pastiche of the views of Booker T. Washington until a slip of the tongue—the word *equality* is used when *responsibility* was intended—arouses hostility and displeasure.

The first reaction of many readers of this chapter must be to wonder if it is rooted in social fact. Did such degenerate events take place in southern American towns in the first half of the twentieth century? One must be careful not to decide the question according to the tabloid rule of thumb that if it is bad enough it must be true. But what would be a reasonable reference point for late twentieth-century North American readers, especially those from cultural and regional backgrounds other than southern? Commentators are one source of possible enlightenment. But even informed opinions vary. Robert O'Meally, for example, in his useful study *The Craft of Ralph Ellison*, is predisposed to take the scene literally, but the evidence he cites both there and in another place is circumstantial and thin.[43] Ellison on the other hand has made a case for reading the scene figuratively, explaining that it was based on a (relatively innocuous) practical joke once played on him involving a coil from an old Model T Ford hooked up to a battery. The whole episode, he says, was "a ritual of initiation. . . . But what my imagination has made of that is the scene in the battle royal where the boys struggle for money on the rug." And in another place he has described the episode in strictly figurative terms as "a ritual in preservation of caste lines, a keeping of taboo to appease the gods and ward off bad luck. It is also the initiation ritual to which all greenhorns are subjected."[44] We have already noted how strongly this authorial explanation has been refuted by Susan Blake, who points out an ideological bias in Ellison's reading of the scene that transforms a social experience into a mythic one. But even without her analysis, many readers of the vividly rendered and painfully palpable battle royal will surely take Ellison's retrospective explanations at a considerable discount.

One is therefore left with unsettled questions concerning the primary meanings and significance of the novel's first chapter. This is by no means a bad thing, for questions of meaning and significance and how they are determined should be on one's mind throughout a reading of the novel. Indeed, they cannot but be on the minds of attentive readers because these very questions are asked within the text by IM, who over and over again is shown trying to discover the import of the very experiences that make up the narrative of the book that the reader of *Invisible Man* holds in his hands. A wholly characteristic attitude of IM is one in which his mind is "grappling for meaning" (chap. 20). In chapter 9, for example, he wonders about the interpretation of a text within the novel's text—the cartman's rendition of the

"Boogie Woogie Blues." "What does it mean, I thought . . . why describe anyone in such contradictory words? . . . Did old Chaplin-
pants, old dusty butt, love her or hate her; or was he merely singing?"
And at the end of chapter 16 there is an extended transcription of IM's
interpretative speculations on the meaning of a text of his own (his
first political speech in the Harlem sports arena), in which at one point
he does what, for better or worse, many readers of *Invisible Man*
surely do at some point: remember something a teacher has said in a
literature class.

The novel's self-conscious concern with the discovery of meaning
is signaled in the first two pages of its very first chapter, which contain
the opening statement of one of the novel's principal motifs: the deathbed utterance of IM's grandfather and his concern to figure out what
the old man meant. Repeated attempts to do so are made by IM
throughout the novel, but even in the epilogue he is still in a state of
uncertainty; the end of his interpretative efforts is in the beginning. "I
could never be sure of what he meant" (chap. 1). Never to be sure of
what is meant is a desirable situation for the reader of *Invisible Man*
to be in, as long as this uncertainty involves no irritable searching after
either facts or symbolic explanations. A state of alert uncertainty is
conducive to an intensified reading experience and a deepened engagement with the text. Such a state, in fact, would seem a precondition of the reader-text collaboration as described by Ellison in 1970.
"Fact and idea must not just be hanging there but must become a
functioning part of the total design, involving itself in the reader as
idea as well as drama. You do this by providing the reader with as
much detail as is possible in terms of the visual *and* the aural, *and* the
rhythmic—to allow him to involve himself, to attach himself, and then
begin to collaborate in the creation of the fictional spell."[45]

If the reader of chapter 1 opens himself to the chapter and collab-
orates in the creation of a spell, in which fact and idea function as
parts of something larger, then he will be off to a very good start with
Invisible Man; he will have been sensitized in a way that allows for
the reciprocal illumination of later episodes by the battle royal and of
the battle royal by later episodes. In chapter 10, when ten drops of

black paint are introduced into a bucket of white paint in order to make it whiter, the reader will recall the ten black youths in the ring at the white man's smoker. In chapter 11, when a group of white medical personnel look on while electric shock therapy is administered to IM, the electrified rug of the first chapter will ping in the reader's memory. When, in chapter 16, IM looks around the dressing room of a Harlem sports arena before his first political speech and notices on the wall a torn photograph of a former prizefight champion, who had "been beaten blind in a crooked fight," the reader will sense more fully than IM himself does why he "felt strangely sad," and the reader will not fail to hear the ping in the image of a game of blindman's buff that is used to describe IM's stumble as he walks to the arena platform. In chapter 17, when he, Clifton, and Ras fight under a Checks-Cashed-Here sign and Ras describes the situation as "three black men fighting in the street because of the white enslaver," IM will not be the only one who remembers and becomes "suddenly alive . . . with the horror of the battle royal." And in chapter 25, in a precise and carefully modulated way, the spectacular account of the Harlem race riot will come into focus as essentially a macrocosmic reenactment of the battle royal.

This and other subtly varied motifs and configurations give *Invisible Man* much of its rhythm and organizational tightness. The motifs become functioning parts of the total design of the novel and furnish both the perimeters, within which the cumulative meanings or significances will be generated, and the coordinates to locate them. To adapt E. K. Brown's useful formulation in his *Rhythm in the Novel*: between the exact repetition of these motifs and their unlimited variation lies the area of significant aesthetic discourse in *Invisible Man*.

Several other motifs are first presented in chapter 1. One of them, already mentioned, is the fierce advice of IM's grandfather, who on his deathbed surprised all his family by revealing that since the Reconstruction he had been "a spy in the enemy's country," and had acquiesced only in appearance to his subservient status as a black. "Live with your head in the lion's mouth," he tells his heirs. "I want you to overcome 'em with yeses, undermine 'em with grins, agree 'em to death and destruction, let 'em swoller you till they vomit or bust wide open." Ellison's 1958 comments on the grandfather are telling.

> There is a good deal of spite in the old man, as there comes to be in his grandson, and the strategy he advises is a kind of jiujitsu of the spirit, a denial and rejection through agreement. Samson, eyeless in Gaza, pulls the building down when his strength returns; politically weak, the grandfather has learned that conformity leads to a similar end, and so advises his children. Thus his mask of meekness conceals the wisdom of one who has learned the secret of saying the "yes" which accomplishes the expressive "no." Here, too, is a rejection of a current code and a denial become metaphysical. More important to the novel is the fact that he represents the ambiguity of the past for the hero, for whom his sphinxlike deathbed advice poses a riddle which points the plot in the dual direction which the hero will follow throughout the novel.[46]

One aspect of this riddle concerns whether the strategy advocated by the grandfather for subverting white power is ultimately effective. As well shall see, it is put to the test in the closing chapters of the novel. Another riddle is also keyed to the grandfather's advice. Why is it, IM wonders, that when he is successful in conforming to the whites' model of Negro subservience, when "he is praised by the most lily-white men of the town" for his conduct, he feels guilty and suspects that what he is doing is "really against the wishes of the white folks" and that what they secretly desire is for him to act "sulky and mean"—that is, to conform to a different white stereotype of Negro behavior. In the very next chapter of *Invisible Man* this riddle will be not so much solved as dramatized and illuminated through Jim Trueblood's account of his relations with both the black and white parts of his southern community.

Another recurring motif instanced in the battle royal chapter concerns black-white sexuality and sexual stereotypes. While the magnificent stark-naked blonde with the round firm breasts, soft thighs, and small American flag tattooed on her belly dances sensuously, the ten black boys are compelled to watch while the white "big shots" yell at them. "Some threatened us if we looked and others if we did not. On my right I saw one boy faint." Another boy is unable to conceal his erection. Commentators rightly speak of the scene in terms of folk motifs concerning black-male sexuality and taboo white women, and of white rituals to effect the symbolic castration of the black male. Similar sexual motifs, taboos, and stereotypes will be encountered in important scenes later in the novel. In one of them, the bedroom scene with the randy redhead Sybil in chapter 24, one of the faintest and subtlest of pings in *Invisible Man* is heard when IM uses Sybil's lipstick to place on her belly, not a small American flag, but the message that she was raped by Santa Claus—another symbol of the white American way.

The last paragraphs of chapter 1 introduce one final motif—"the crude joke that kept me running," as IM later calls it (epilogue). In the dream IM has on the night after the battle royal, his grandfather tells him to open the briefcase he has been presented at the conclusion of his speech. Instead of finding his scholarship, IM finds an official envelope, inside of which is another envelope and another and another, until he finally comes to one that when opened is found to contain an engraved document reading, To Whom It May Concern: Keep This Nigger-Boy Running. The sociohistorical root of this dream is the cruel practical joke that has its antecedents in the days of slavery, when illiterate blacks needed a note signed by the white master in order to travel from plantation to plantation. A Negro greenhorn looking for work is told by a prospective white employer to try at another white business and is given a sealed letter to carry to the next prospective employer. But the same scenario follows again and again until it is realized that each letter contains the same terse message: Keep This Nigger-Boy Running.[47] His college scholarship is not the last piece of paper given IM by whites that contains information or a message ultimately reducible to the brutal simplicity of this joke's punch line. After the battle royal, the next hoop through which IM is made to jump is the Negro college, and the next papers he is given are from its president, a white surrogate.

5

CHAPTERS 2–6

Did you ever dream lucky, then wake up cold in hand?
Did you ever dream lucky, then wake up cold in hand?
Billy Banks, "Baldheaded Mama"

This section of *Invisible Man* covers the events of a single spring day during IM's third year at college—a day that unexpectedly turns out to be his last as a student. There are four principal *mise-en-scènes:* a black sharecropper's log cabin, its chinks filled with chalk-white clay, the earth around its porch "hard and white from where wash water had long been thrown"; a bar/brothel called the Golden Day—a cluster of "sun-shrunk shacks at the railroad crossing where the disabled veterans visited the whores"; the college chapel, with its rows of "straight and torturous benches" facing a platform with a pulpit and a rail of polished brass, behind which rise the banked rows of the choir and organ pipes stretching to the ceiling; and, finally, the office of the college president, with its old heavy furnishings and its "framed portrait photographs and relief plaques of presidents and industrialists, men of power—fixed like trophies or heraldic emblems upon the walls." Like the settings, the characters and the incidents in chapters

2 to 6 are new. But the themes and motifs, and the inner dynamics of situations, are to a considerable extent elaborations of material first adumbrated in the prologue and chapter 1.

LOG CABIN

Chapter 2 is dominated by the magnificently realized figure of Jim Trueblood, who is characterized almost entirely through his own voice and words and who tells his own story just as he tells other stories, "with a sense of humor and a magic that made them come alive." Trueblood is not the only important character in the chapter, however. Like so much else in *Invisible Man,* chapter 2 turns on the contrast of black and white—in this case, that of the dirt-poor southern black sharecropper and Mr. Norton, the Boston millionaire and philanthropist. The two figures are contrasted from the ground up: Norton's custom-made, white, trimmed-with-black shoes have the "elegantly slender, well-bred appearance of fine gloves" in comparison with Trueblood's "cheap tan brogues." In the main, however, compared with the earthy sharecropper, who is the most compelling and vividly rendered single character in *Invisible Man,* both the character and the characterization of Mr. Norton seem distinctly thin. Unlike Trueblood and most of the novel's other leading characters, for example, he has no distinctive verbal signature. Nor is he made more substantial during his subsequent appearances. In chapter 3, although he is the center of the narrator's attention during the uproar at the Golden Day, he is unconscious most of the time and functions as a comic prop. And when he reappears unexpectedly in the epilogue—IM recounts an improbable meeting with him in the New York subway—the brief scene is a clinker. It is the one inert spot in the epilogue and one of the very few aesthetic miscalculations in the entire novel.

This being so, the reader of *Invisible Man* would be well advised to read Mr. Norton's conversation with IM in the opening pages of chapter 2 as carefully as possible. For the more sharply Mr. Norton can be brought into focus and the more depth his presentation can be felt to have, the more powerful will be the contrast between him and Trueblood and the stronger and more gripping the reader's felt sense of the dark symbiosis between sharecropper and millionaire. The hidden affinity is the incest wish—the desire of the father for the sexual possession of the daughter. The attraction-repulsion dynamics of this affinity are all the more powerfully present in the text because they are nowhere explicitly mentioned. It is all showing and no telling because the narrative point of view is restricted to that of the character IM, who has no idea why Mr. Norton listens so intently to Trueblood's story ("Something was going on which I didn't get"; "What was wrong with Mr. Norton anyway, why should he get *that* upset over Trueblood?"). The most important effect of the affinity never being made explicit is to intensify the reader's engagement with the text, through allowing him to make connections not visible on the surface. This recuperative activity is further encouraged by the attenuation of the above-the-surface presentation of Mr. Norton, which from the point of view of reader involvement could be regarded as a deliberate authorial calculation.

One of the first things Mr. Norton tells IM as they begin their ill-fated drive into the country is, "I know my life rather well." One gets another whiff of smugness and self-satisfaction when he tells IM that he knew the founder. "He was my friend and I believed in his vision. So much so, that sometimes I don't know whether it was his vision or mine." Norton's work for the college over the years, he says, has been a "pleasant fate." Philanthropy, as Thoreau observed during his withering analysis of the subject at the end of the first chapter of *Walden,* "is almost the only virtue which is sufficiently appreciated by mankind. Nay, it is greatly overrated; and it is our selfishness which overrates it."[48] Certainly one senses an underlying selfishness, an egotistical gratification, in Mr. Norton's paternalistic attitude toward the Negro college. He speaks of his comfortable "feeling that your people were somehow connected with my destiny. That what happened to you was connected with what would happen to me. . . . Yes, you are my fate, young man. Only you can tell me what it really is." His "real life's work," he says, has been spent in helping the college; that is, in his "first-hand organizing of human life." One might well recall these reflections when reading in chapter 10 about the "optic white" paint that is made even whiter by the addition of a certain number of drops of black paint. And by the time Mr. Norton repeats that "I am dependent upon you to learn my fate," the reader may well have come to feel that he is really practicing a kind of psychological exploitation disguised as other-regarding benevolence.

Mr. Norton goes on to speak of a "more important, more passionate, and, yes, even more sacred" reason than all the others for his philanthropic involvement with Negroes: the memory of his dead daughter. When he does so, one might again recall the first chapter of *Walden:* "The philanthropist too often surrounds mankind with the remembrance of his own cast-off griefs as an atmosphere, and calls it sympathy."[49] Mr. Norton shows IM a tinted miniature of his daughter, whom he describes in insipidly idealizing terms ("A delicate flower that bloomed in the liquid light of the moon. A nature not of this world"). He then recalls how, she being "too pure and too good and too beautiful" for life, their world-tour *à deux* was interrupted by her illness and death. It is shortly after this that Mr. Norton notices a log cabin and, upon hearing that the two visibly pregnant women washing clothes in the yard are a mother and daughter who have both been impregnated by the same husband/father, says that he "must talk" with this man and clambers out of the car "as though compelled by some pressing urgency."

What the reader of *Invisible Man* comes to learn from Mr. Norton's reaction to Trueblood, and to his story of how he came to commit incest with his daughter, is that the white millionaire is far from knowing his life "rather well"; that black involvement in his fate is at a deeper and darker level than he fondly thinks; that his idealization of his daughter has a sexual substratum; and that his philanthropy is contaminated not only by selfishness but also by a kind of voyeurism. In bringing this recognition into focus, it is helpful to recall the end of chapter 4 of Freud's *Civilization and Its Discontents*. The sexual life of civilized man, says Freud, is severely impaired. One reason for the impairment is that the economic structure of society influences the amount of sexual freedom available to a person. The laws of economic necessity require of an individual the expenditure of a large amount of psychic energy, which perforce has to be withdrawn from sexuality. This restrictive tendency on the part of civilization was apparent even in "its first, totemic phase" in which one already finds "the prohibition against an incestuous choice of object." This is, observes Freud, perhaps "the most drastic mutilation which man's erotic life has in all time experienced."[50] This primal taboo, one may say, is so deeply inscribed in the civilized psyche that it can come to be seen as a supernatural interdiction. Certainly it seems so to Mr. Norton when he shouts at Trueblood, "You did and are unharmed!" with "his blue eyes blazing into the black face with something like envy and indignation." "You have looked upon chaos and are not destroyed! . . . You feel no inner turmoil, no need to cast out the offending eye?"

Jim Trueblood's answer to Mr. Norton is unforgettable. "I'm all right, suh. My eyes is all right too. And when I feels po'ly in my gut I takes a little soda and it goes away." In beginning to tell the story of the recent events that have so changed his life, Trueblood first describes the differing ways in which local blacks and local whites responded to the news of his disgrace, though he does not comprehend the underlying reason for the differences: "'stead of things gittin' bad they got better. The nigguhs up at the school don't like me, but the white folks treats me fine." The former have tried to get Trueblood and his family to move "clean outta the county" because the sharecropper does not conform to the sanitized image of the humble hardworking Negro who knows his place, on the maintenance of which depends the continued financial support of wealthy northern whites. The local southern whites, on the other hand, "gimme more help than they ever give any other colored man, no matter how good a nigguh he was," even though "I done the worse thing a man could ever do in his family." These whites, of course, are pleased to have such a good example of the degraded and sexually promiscuous nature of Negro life to reinforce their racial prejudices. (One remembers IM noting in the previous chapter that when he was praised for his conduct by white men he always felt strangely guilty because of his nagging feeling that his actions really went "against the wishes of the white folks.")

Trueblood then goes on to tell the extraordinary story of how he came to penetrate his daughter. This virtuoso recital demands close examination. Trueblood begins by explaining how the combination of poverty and cold forces him and his wife and daughter to sleep together for warmth. As he lies in the dark, smelling fat meat from the stove and worrying "'bout my family, how they was goin' to eat and all," he hears his daughter say "Daddy" softly and low and knows she is thinking not of her father but of the boy who has been hanging around her. He then begins to think about a girl called Margaret he used to have back in Mobile who would say "Daddy" to him in the middle of the night as they lay together listening to the sounds of the boats on the river—sounds that Trueblood describes in two splendidly fresh visual images, both of which have a sweetly erotic suggestiveness: the young juicy melon "split wide open a-layin' all spread out and cool and sweet on top of all the green striped ones"; and "the gal in a red dress . . . plump and juicy and kinda switchin' her tail 'cause she knows you watchin' and you *know* she know."

In her sleep, Matty Lou, the daughter, says "Daddy" again and, mistaking her father for that boy, moves over against him. Realizing that his daughter has become a woman, Trueblood moves away but then drops into a dream—a dream from which he will awake to find himself engaged in sexual intercourse with Matty Lou. Primarily but not exclusively sexual in its referents, the dream is richly suggestive in connection both with Trueblood and his incestuous act and with the larger thematic concerns of chapter 2. To say this, however, presupposes an interpretative determination that responsibility for the dream is to be assigned not only to the dreamer (the character Jim Trueblood) but also to the narrator and/or the implied author of *Invisible Man*. This is a slightly more complex variant of the discriminations (discussed in the previous chapter) that the reader of *Invisible Man* has to make between IM the character and IM the narrator. Trueblood's dream, that is to say, can be interpreted both literally (as an expression or showing forth of the character's below-the-surface psychic levels) and symbolically (that is, as an expression of the preoccupations of the narrator/author of the text, of which the character Jim Trueblood is a part).

The dream opens with the dreamer in search of "some fat meat." The "white folks downtown" refer him to Mr. Broadnax, who lives in a big house on a hill. When he gets there, the dreamer enters through the front door even though he knows it is a forbidden entrance for blacks. Another taboo is broken when he enters "a big white bedroom" smelling strongly of woman. In a corner of the room is a tall grandfather clock, from which steps a white woman dressed in "a nightgown of soft white silky stuff and nothin' else." She screams and holds him tight; he is scared to touch her because she is white. He throws her on the bed and they struggle. Then a door opens and Mr. Broadnax's voice is heard to say: "They just nigguhs, leave 'em do it."

To this point at least, it is hard not to regard the dream as primarily narratorial/authorial. This is the unspoken assumption of Houston Baker, who interprets the dream as a "parodic allegory," which together with the entire Trueblood episode "can be read as a pejorative commentary on the castrating effects of white philanthropy." Mr. Broadnax is glossed as "Mr. Broad-in-acts"—a white philanthropist whose hill stands for the North and whose altruism toward blacks has a sexual and racist substratum.[51] From this point of view, Mr. Broadnax's remark about the fornicators being "just nigguhs" is a demotic echo of Mr. Norton's more genteely phrased reflection on hearing that the younger of the two pregnant women washing clothes in the yard is unmarried: "But that shouldn't be so strange. I understand that your people—Never mind."

The remainder of the dream, however, clearly should be assigned to Trueblood. Once he frees himself from the scantily clad white woman, the dreamer's search for fat meat leads him to the grandfather clock. Once he begins to enter the clock, the imagery becomes unmistakably suggestive of the penetration, leading to orgasm, that is simultaneously occurring between Trueblood and Matty Lou. The door of the clock has "some kinda crinkly stuff like steel wool on the facing." Inside is a hot, dark tunnel, at the end of which the dreamer comes to see a bright light "like a jack-o-lantern over a graveyard." The light gets brighter and brighter as the dreamer approaches; when he is right up against it, "it burst like a great big electric light in my eyes and scalded me all over."

Trueblood wakes to find himself in the middle of coitus, from which it is not a simple matter to disengage himself. "She didn't want me to go then—and to tell the honest-to-God truth I found out that I didn't want to go neither." He then hears his wife Kate scream. Her frenzied response to the discovery of her husband's act is described in slow motion. She threatens to shoot him with his own double-barreled shotgun, while he tries vainly to explain that his was an unconscious "dream-sin." She then takes up an ax and wounds him badly with it before dropping it and vomiting. Trueblood, who has determined to take his punishment but is unable to keep from moving his head away as the ax falls, subsequently tries to explain what has happened to neighbors and to his preacher; but he is ostracized by both. He goes away alone and broods about his simultaneous guilt and nonguilt "until I thinks my brain go'n bust." Finally, one night, "way early in the morning," he looks up at the stars and starts to sing. He begins with a church song, but emotional release only begins to come when he starts singing the blues: "I sings me some blues that night ain't never been sang before." During his singing he makes up his mind to return home regardless of the consequences.

Norton's reaction to Trueblood's story is deeply destabilizing. He listens intently, ignoring IM's pleas to leave. By the story's end his face has been drained of color. He looks ghostly as he stares into the sharecropper's face. He then removes his wallet from his pocket—the miniature of his daughter is inadvertently removed as well, "but he did not look at it this time"—and gives Trueblood a one-hundred-dollar bill. The detumescent visage, the unlooked-at miniature, and the cash payment all suggest that Norton's obsessive interest in Trueblood's story is rooted in his own forbidden sexual feelings for his daughter, which have been vicariously satisfied through his intense participation in Trueblood's incestuous coupling—the illiterate and uncivilized black having acted out the white man's repressed sexual desires.

The other member of Trueblood's audience, the character IM, has a different reaction to the story. He is torn between humiliation and fascination, and experiences "a sense of shame" which, one may assume, is the same as that felt by other members of the college community. But it should by no means be the reaction of the reader of *Invisible Man*. Trueblood's act of incest is precipitated by his impoverished economic condition, which forces husband, wife, and eldest child to sleep together for warmth, and by the afterglow of his fulfilling sexual life with Margaret back in Mobile. One can certainly reflect that the presence of a white woman in his dream suggests that Trueblood's sexual desires are more complex and more affected by black-white dynamics than his reputation as a good family man and his sweet memories of Mobile might suggest. But Ellison's novel is not Faulkner's *Absalom, Absalom!*. In *Invisible Man*, miscegenation and incest are separable categories. And in any event, from the point of view of character, the most important aspect of Trueblood's transgression is his response to it.

Joseph Frank has written very well of Dostoyevski's and Ellison's shared ability to depict in an unsparing way "the unforgivable and unredeemable, and yet [to] manage to do so in a manner that affirms the humanity of the people involved rather than negat[es] it."[52] During his night of blues singing, Jim Trueblood makes up his mind that "I ain't nobody but myself and ain't nothing I can do but let whatever is gonna happen, happen"; he returns home because "I'm a man and man don't leave his family." This instinctive concern, a moving reaffirmation of elemental human values and bonds, is the antithesis of Mr. Norton's sentimental mishmash about fate and destiny, and his philanthropic pseudoinvolvement in Negro life. Jim Trueblood is like that boss quail he mentions early in his story. When the dark comes and the "boss bird" tries to get his covey together again, he whistles softly and moves softly toward where he knows the quail hunter waits with his gun. "Still he got to round them up, so he keeps on comin'. Them boss quails is like a good man, what he got to do he *do*."

BROTHEL

Chapter 3 of *Invisible Man* offers the reader a kind of entertainment very different from Jim Trueblood's "autobiographical chronicle of personal catastrophe expressed lyrically," to recall Ralph Ellison's description of the blues form. The account of the goings-on at the Golden Day is a rollicking, madcap comedy—a Marx Brothers– or Goon Show–type entertainment, in which the comedy team is a group of mentally disturbed veterans who are masters of the put-on, players of "some vast and complicated game . . . whose goal was laughter and whose rules and subtleties I [the character IM] could never grasp." One player does a drum-major routine, using his cane as a baton, but when a car approaches he instantly slips into the role of a tough-talking military policeman at a checkpoint. Two other players use Mr. Norton's arrival at the Golden Day as the basis for an impromptu send-up:

> "Gentlemen, this man is my grandfather!"
> "But he's *white*, his name's Norton."
> "I should know my own grandfather! He's Thomas Jefferson and I'm his grandson—on the 'field-nigger' side," the tall man said.
> "Sylvester, I do believe that you're right. I certainly do," he said, staring at Mr. Norton. "Look at those features. Exactly like yours—from the identical mold. Are you sure he didn't spit you upon the earth, fully clothed?"
> "No, no, that was my father," the man said earnestly.

Another player, the bartender Halley, also uses American racial inequalities as the basis of a brief skit—his straight-faced exchange with

Chapters 2–6

IM concerning Mr. Norton's admissibility to the Golden Day: "He too good to come in? Tell him we don't Jimcrow nobody."

Broader comic exchanges and situations are also found in this chapter. There is the hilarious discussion between two whores concerning the sexual potency of the elderly Mr. Norton, who lies unconscious on the bed next to them:

> "He's kinda cute," she said. "Just like a little white baby."
> "What kinda ole baby?" the small skinny girl asked.
> "That's the kind, an *ole* baby."
> "You just like white men, Edna. That's all," the skinny one said.
> Edna shook her head and smiled as though amused at herself. "I sho' do. I just love 'em. Now this one, old as he is, he could put his shoes under my bed any night."
> "Shucks, me I'd kill an old man like that."
> "Kill him nothing," Edna said. "Girl, don't you know that all these rich ole white men got monkey glands and billy goat balls? These ole bastards don't never git enough. They want to have the whole world."
> . . . .
> "It's the truth," Edna said. "I used to have me one in Chicago—"
> "Now you ain't never been to no Chicago, gal," the other one interrupted.
> "How you know I ain't? Two years ago . . . Shucks, you don't know nothing. That old white man right there might have him a coupla jackass balls!"

And there is the chapter's centerpiece, the overthrow of Supercargo, the authority figure, and the ensuing carnival atmosphere of misrule in which the anarchic energies of the vets find flamboyant expression as social interdictions are transgressed. Mr. Norton's face is slapped by a black hand and he is spoken to in a way that IM knows can only bring trouble when order is restored, but which nonetheless gives him "a fearful satisfaction."

When the comic energies of the chapter have waned, however, readers of *Invisible Man* may well wonder whether the social content of the chapter—the mentally disturbed vets—is appropriate material for farcical treatment and comic exploitation. What is so funny, one might well ask, about the plight of dispossessed members of the Negro middle class—"doctors, lawyers, teachers, Civil Service workers," a composer, a chemist with a Phi Beta Kappa key—who have been broken on the rack of white American society? Take the story of the short fat vet, a medical specialist who had served in France during World War I with the Army Medical Corps, had remained abroad after the Armistice to study, and then had returned to practice in America, where, "for saving a human life," he was taken out at midnight by ten men in masks and beaten with whips.

Since the Golden Day chapter is not the only section of *Invisible Man* to raise the question of the appropriateness of a comic treatment of a deeply serious subject, the matter deserves consideration at this point. In a later chapter I shall have something to say about the comic vision and comic form of *Invisible Man*. The subject here, however, is the novel's broadly humorous, and sometimes farcically low-comedy, treatment of situations that provoke, not the reflective intellectual laughter of high comedy, but something much more visceral and side-splitting. The first point to make is that in *Invisible Man*, owing to the high degree of artistic elaboration of its material, there can be as much food for thought, as much reflective depth, in broadly comic situations as in more seriously treated ones. Take, for example, the zany Freudian overlay in chapter 3—a kind of slapstick expressionism in which the attendant Supercargo, a black giant of a man who usually wears a hard-starched white uniform, obviously stands for the superego and its tyrannical repression of the aggressive energies of the id—that is, of the vets. "We're patients sent here as therapy," says one of the vets, "But they sent along an attendant, a kind of censor, to see that the therapy fails." Another says, "Sometimes I get so afraid of him that I feel he's inside my head." This overlay might simply be considered a little extra icing on the comic cake. But if one reflects on its implications in light of the Norton-Trueblood dynamics in the previous chapter, and those of the smoker episode in Chapter 1, it can be seen as a brilliantly suggestive encapsulation of the Freudian pyschic dynamic as played out on the American socioracial scene. To quote again from the fourth chapter of *Civilization and Its Discontents:* "Civilization behaves towards sexuality as a people or a stratum of its population does which has subjected another one to its exploitation. Fear of a revolt by the suppressed elements drives it to stricter precautionary measures."[53]

The second and more general point is that broad comedy with a pronounced ethnic/racial component is a distinctive (perhaps *the* distinctive) manifestation of American humor. When its relationship to American society is understood, the appropriateness, even the inevitability, of its employment in a serious imaginative exploration of black-white relationships becomes clear. The most helpful text in making this connection is an address entitled "American Humor" that Ellison gave at Oklahoma State University in April 1970. There was a certain kind of comedy, Ellison argued, that seemed to be nothing less than "the basic American mode in literature":

> [The] sense of the uncertainty plus the possibility afforded by this country, by its natural wealth, and by its growing, by the diversity of its regions and of its people, made for the need of a humor which would, first, allow us to deal with the unexpected; and, second, allow us to adjust to one another in our diversity. The northerner found the southerner strange. The southerner found the northerner despicable. The blacks found the whites peculiar. The whites found the blacks ridiculous. And you know how it goes. Some agency had to be adopted which would allow us to live with one another without destroying one another, and the agency was laughter—was humor. . . . If you can laugh at me, you don't have to kill me. If I can laugh at you, I don't have to kill you.

According to Ellison, Negro humor became part of mainstream American humor "precisely because there is no one who sees the absurd . . . more than the person who has lived closest to it. A great deal of the style of American humor came out of the black experience. . . . It came because we could not escape the absurdity, the philosophical absurdity of the racial arrangements within the society." Some of the absurd situations were painful, "but *it is precisely because they are so painful that they have to be comic* [italics mine]. The situations call forth the comedy, out of the need not to be destroyed." Ellison went on to recall that when *Invisible Man* was published in the early 1950s, white friends found the number of comic situations in the novel puzzling and could not understand the appropriateness of such treatment. But Ellison, who described his sense of the comic as coming "out of the tradition of my own people here, their own variation on the American theme of comedy," had intended his novel "to be funny."[54]

At the end of chapter 3, the "short, fat, very intelligent-looking" vet who had been a medical specialist gives IM some advice, on which he has the opportunity to elaborate at the beginning of chapter 7, when both men find themselves heading north on the same bus. But before IM can begin to understand this advice, and begins to understand the contradictions that have made the educated vets into mental patients, he first has to learn a great deal about the black college that has provided him with "the only identity I had ever known."

COLLEGE

In the short fourth chapter of *Invisible Man*, which describes his return to the college from the Golden Day, IM at one point reflects that he believes in "the principles of the Founder with all my heart and soul." Who was the founder of the college and what were his principles? The answer, inferable from the details of the text, is that the founder is Booker T. Washington and the college is the Tuskegee Institute in Alabama, which Ralph Ellison attended for three years before leaving for New York at the end of his junior year (just as IM does). The statue of the founder on which IM the narrator remarks at the beginning of chapter 2, for example, is found on the campus of the Institute. The inscription at its base reads: "Booker T. Washington 1856–1915. He lifted the veil of ignorance from his people and pointed the way to progress through education and industry."⁵⁵ Most of those who have seen the statue will remember with an aesthetic shudder the garish iconography of the thick-lipped barefoot black savage crouched under a veil held by a lighter skinned (Washington was half white), erect-standing, and fully acculturated gentleman wearing laced shoes, a three-piece suit, and a bow tie.

Washington was the most influential Negro leader of his generation. His basic views were outlined in his 1895 address delivered at the opening of the Cotton States and International Exposition in Atlanta—it is from this address that IM quotes in the speech he makes at the smoker in chapter 1. The keystone of Washington's program was that Negroes must renounce social equality as a goal and accept white supremacy as a precondition of their attaining an improved economic position, which would result from humble and industrious living within the framework of southern segregation. Together with industry, education was the key to Negro improvement. The institute Washington founded in Tuskegee was originally chartered as a normal school to train black teachers, and much of the other training it offered was vocational. And of course it attempted to inculcate in its students Washington's ideology. The Institute's financial dependence on northern white money continued into the time of Robert Russa Moton, the handpicked successor of Washington (though in the early 1920s the Institute was financially sound enough to be able to give a portion of its land to the Veterans Administration for the construction of a hospital). In November 1933, two years before his retirement and some weeks after the young Ralph Ellison had arrived on campus, President Moton delivered an address in the college chapel in which he recalled his last, deathbed conversation with Washington.⁵⁶

It is toward the fictional counterpart of this chapel that IM is walking at the beginning of chapter 5. The opening pages of this chapter are an attempt on the part of the narrator IM to encapsulate in eight paragraphs the essence of the more emotionally evocative, and therefore memorable, experiences of his younger self over the course of his three collegiate years—a period of time to which novelists writ-

INVISIBLE MAN

ing in a more conventionally realistic mode would have devoted scores of pages. This kind of compression, which inevitably moves in the direction of poetic intensity and expressionistic distortions, is dramatically and psychologically appropriate, in that it suggests—implicitly it even mimes—the high-strung emotional state of IM the character, who by this point in his long day of disasters is full of foreboding that his mishaps with Mr. Norton may result in expulsion from the college and the shattering of his identity. The minatory intensity of his preoccupations is registered in the opening paragraph, not only by the moon, "a white man's bloodshot eye," but also by the whitewashed stones, which seem "cryptic messages" for those heading for the chapel.

In the following paragraphs, it is mainly through aural recollections that IM's memories are focused and evoked: there are the sweet Christmas sounds of the organ and trombone choir "speaking carols to the distances drifted with snow"; there is the lulling movement of the multisyllabic words of the sermons delivered in the college chapel—"smooth articulate tones" so unlike the wild emotion of the "crude preachers" most of the students had known in their home towns; and there is the equally impressive remembered sound of IM's own voice. A long, italicized paragraph evokes a member of the appreciative chapel audience listening to the rhetorical skills of IM the student leader. She is the gray-haired matron Miss Susie Gresham who, as IM's spasm of intense recollection mounts, becomes transformed through the intensity of his need for roots, for an identity, into a black earth mother—"aged, of slavery, yet bearer of something warm and vital and all-enduring."

The one other paragraph-long memory in the opening of chapter 5 raises an interesting question. The subject of this simultaneously elliptical and overwritten passage is the implacably hostile southern whites "who trailed their words to us through blood and violence and ridicule and condescension with drawling smiles" and who are so much more important determinants in the lives of southern blacks than are northern philanthropists. The intensity of the emotion IM

feels is conveyed in a torrential sentence of Faulknerian rhetorical complexity concerning these men, "who as they talked, aroused furtive visions within me of blood-froth sparkling their chins like their familiar tobacco juice, and upon their lips the curdled milk of a million black slave mammies' withered dugs, a treacherous and fluid knowledge of our being, imbibed at our source and now regurgitated foul upon us." The question is why, especially given the intensity of IM's feelings, this fundamentally important aspect of American Negro experience is not more fully represented in *Invisible Man*.

One might speculate that the calculation was made that there was already enough density and weight in the southern chapters of the novel and that any more would have made a perceived disproportion between its southern and its New York segments. One might further speculate that by the late 1940s the southern white racist and his treatment of the Negro was no longer a particularly fresh fictional subject. It is also the case that the virtual omission of this aspect of southern reality from *Invisible Man* makes for a less depressing and less deterministic context in which to place the story of the development of a young Negro who, in the story's epilogue, will be found speaking in upbeat tones about the manifold possibilities of American life. Finally, one might find shelter in generic considerations and observe that since the hostility of southern white racists is something that IM the character feels in his bones, he does not have to learn about it during the course of his development. This being so, one could argue that there is no reason why the topic should figure in a bildungsroman, a development-novel centered on what its protagonist has to learn about himself and the world he lives in during the crucially formative years of his late youth.

The centerpiece of chapter 5 is the speech in the college chapel delivered by the Reverend Homer A. Barbee. The speech is a eulogy for the founder; but it is important to realize that it is just as much about Dr. Bledsoe, his appointed successor and the current president of the college, whom Barbee calls "the co-architect of a great and noble experiment." Nor should one fail to notice the subtle suggestions that Barbee and Bledsoe are a composite figure whose identities and functions blur together. For one thing, there is the similarity in the appearance of their names. For another, there is the cinemalike overlay, in which, at one point during his speech, Barbee describes how on an earlier occasion, when the founder fainted, Bledsoe had taken control of an audience by using the very rhetorical techniques Barbee is himself at that moment employing. And finally, there is the unmistakably telling notation of IM's difficulty in seeing Barbee when the latter first rises to speak. "My eyes had focused only upon the white men and Dr. Bledsoe. So that now as he [Barbee] arose and crossed slowly to the center of the platform, I had the notion that part of Dr. Bledsoe had risen and moved forward, leaving his other part smiling in the chair."

Barbee's eulogy takes the form of a mythic narrative of the life of a culture hero, a redemptive figure, the ritual remembrance of whom renews in the hearts of his followers the dream of a special destiny and feeds their hunger for transcendence. The founder is compared to Moses leading his people out of bondage, and, since the path to the promised land leads through an educational institution, he is also—somewhat bizarrely—identified as a "black Aristotle." But the principal analogy, of course, is to Christ. Barbee's speech is in essence a two-act pageant commemorating the birth (and early days) and the death of the hero—these two liminal moments being not only the most affecting passages in the hero's life cycle but also the two points where it is easiest to work in supernatural overtones and biblical resonances. This narrative is presented as a "true story of rich implication, [a] living parable." To the dark and barren land, hungry for deliverance, comes "a humble prophet, lowly like the humble carpenter of Nazareth," whose life at one point is saved by a possibly providential intervention ("we must not rule out the possibility of an emissary direct from above"). In the second panel of the diptych, the hero's passage to death coincides with the ascent of a mountain and is placed against the celestial background of a great sun setting; death is at the mountain summit; the form of apotheosis is "a single jewel-like star" against

the now black sky; and the dying Founder's final act is the anointing
of a successor, who will be a token of the hero's resurrection "if not
in the flesh, in the spirit. And in a sense in the flesh too. For has not
your present leader [Bledsoe] become his living agent, his physical
presence?"

Like the rest of the chapel audience, the character IM is deeply
moved by the expert rhetorical manipulations of Barbee, who plays
"upon the whole audience without the least show of exertion." So
powerful is the cumulative effect that IM comes to feel guilty over the
Norton fiasco, and to accept his guilt. "For although I had not intended it, any act that endangered the continuity of the dream was an
act of treason." The reaction of the reader of *Invisible Man* to Barbee's
speech, however, is quite different. For one thing, IM the narrator has
placed the speech in a frame that puts the reader at a critical distance
from it. Before the speech begins, the retrospective narrator has already caustically spoken of the chapel stage as the place where "the
black rite of Horatio Alger was performed to God's own acting
script"; and at the end of the speech there is the incident we have
already discussed: Barbee's pratfall and the revelation that he is blind.

Even without these tip-offs, the careful reader of *Invisible Man*
should be able to realize that Barbee's speech undermines itself from
within through its banality of language, tired tropes, and cheap rhetorical tricks. These are all the more immediately glaring if one's ear
retains as a point of comparison the performance of Trueblood, another skilled rhetorician. Trueblood's earthy and colorful speech vivi-
fies and authenticates his discourse; and it is memorable—like the
simile of the jaybird "that the yellow jackets done stung 'til he's par-
alyzed" that IM recalls hundreds of pages later at the end of his novel's
last chapter. Barbee's speech, on the other hand, is laced with hack-
neyed similes and allusions, and autodidactic flourishes. A message
falls "like a seed on fallow ground"; fear and hatred are crouched "like
a demon waiting to spring." Other examples include: "a *coup-de-
grace*, as the French would say"; "at our throats already we felt the
cold hands of sorrow"; "we looked with bated breath into . . ."; "that

old slavery smell, worse than the rank halitosis of hoary death." Barbee's purple rhetoric, which leaves no trace on IM's memory, seems only to move leadenly toward a bogus transcendence, as grotesque as the illusion created by his rhythmic rocking during his oration. Barbee would tilt forward and fall back "until it seemed that his head floated free of his body and was held close to it only by the white band of his collar."

Barbee's speech is further demystified in chapter 6, in which Dr. Bledsoe, anointed successor, coarchitect of the dream, and Barbee's double, is revealed in his true nature. Before his collegiate day of reckoning, IM had regarded Bledsoe as "the example of everything I hoped to be." But now the cumulative significance of a number of specific notations begins to become clear. Before meeting a white benefactor, Bledsoe composes his features in a mirror until his face becomes a bland mask; he refuses to eat in the dining hall with visiting whites and stands hat in hand when he addresses them after dinner; he has the knack of looking humble even when in formal dress—those baggy trousers and ill-fitting coat; and he has the trick of making himself seem smaller than his white guests even though he is physically larger. What all of these details suggest is that Bledsoe, as he himself says in chapter 6, knows how "to act the nigger."

What IM learns during his interview with him in chapter 6 is that behind this subservient mask Bledsoe is actually manipulating the white benefactors for his own advantage. The college and its ideals, like the myth of the founder, are so much eyewash, and no black with any brains would believe in them for a moment: "Why, the dumbest black bastard in the cotton patch knows that the only way to please a white man is to tell him a lie! What kind of education are you getting around here . . . you don't even know the difference between the way things are and the way they're supposed to be. My God, what is the race coming to?" Bledsoe goes on to explain that everything is a matter of power politics. The white folks have the power and if you want to share in it you have to tell them the kind of lie they want to hear: "This is a power set-up, son, and I'm at the controls. . . . When you buck against me, you're bucking against power, rich white folk's power, the nation's power—which means government power!" Bledsoe's whole career at the college has been all about "telling white folks how to think about the things I know about."

What the college really is, Bledsoe says in effect, is an institutionalization of the deathbed advice of IM's grandfather. It is no wonder, then, that after he leaves the president's office IM suddenly feels that "my grandfather was hovering over me, grinning triumphantly out of the dark." But IM cannot allow himself to accept the implications of this feeling—to admit that his grandfather had made sense. To do so would be for this ambitious youth to lose the only identity he has ever known. As he reflects, he knows "no other way of living" and knows of no "other forms of success available to such as me." He must will himself to believe that Bledsoe knows best in sending him away from the college, and he must accept at face value the letters of introduction to northern benefactors of the college. The next morning he is on a bus to New York, where the rest of *Invisible Man* is set.

6

CHAPTERS 7–11

I went to an employment office
Got a number and I got in line
They called everybody's number
But they never did call mine.

They say if you's white, should be all right
If you's brown, stick around
But as you're black
Mmm, Mmm, Brother, git back, git back, git back.
> Big Bill Broonzy, "Black, Brown, and White"

During their interview in chapter 6, Dr. Bledsoe had questioned IM about the strange-talking vet, the doctor-turned-patient whom he had met at the Golden Day. "I'll have to investigate him," Bledsoe had said. "A Negro like that should be under lock and key." It is because the college president has arranged for the vet's speedy removal from the vicinity of the college that IM finds him at the back of the segregated bus he boards the next morning. As they travel north, the vet resumes his analysis of IM. At the Golden Day he had diagnosed him as someone who failed to understand "the simple facts of life. . . . He registers with his senses but short-circuits his brain. . . . Behold! a walking zombie! Already he's learned to repress not only his emotions but his humanity. He's invisible, a walking personification of the Negative." The vet's prescription for this condition, offered during the bus ride, is critical self-understanding rooted in an accurate knowledge of the world. "For God's sake, learn to look beneath the surface," he tells IM. "Play the game, but don't believe in it . . . learn how it operates, learn how *you* operate." The crucial insight, the vet goes on to say, is for the young Negro to recognize his invisibility: "You're hidden right out in the open—that is, you would be if you only realized it. They wouldn't see you because they don't expect you to know anything." From this recognition, the vet says, opportunity and possibility follow. His last words of advice to IM are: "Be your own father, young man. And remember, the world is possibility if only you'll discover it."

At this early point in his story, IM has hardly reached the stage of development where the recognition of invisibility and the possibilities it confers is psychologically possible. But while he still clings to the blinkered identity the college offers him, he is able to respond to the vet's paean to New York as "a dream," a place that offers freedom and possibility to aspiring black Americans. Indeed, when IM enters Harlem, "a city-within-a-city," for the first time at the end of chapter 7, he appropriates the vet's very phrases in identifying it as a place made not "of realities but of dreams . . . a new world of possibility suggested itself to me." What IM does not remember, however, are the ironic undertones and cynical qualifications in the vet's rhetoric. IM's northern freedom would have to be symbolic, the vet had remarked, and would probably take the form of any man's most easily accessible symbol of freedom: a woman. And there was a grim implication in his encapsulation of the northward movement of southern blacks. "Now all the little black boys run away to New York. Out of the fire into the melting pot."

As the vet intimates, IM's journey north has a representative sociohistorical dimension. Indeed, the migration from the rural South to the urban industrialized North has been the most important demographic fact of black American experience in the twentieth century. The Negro population of New York, for example, grew from ninety-two thousand in 1910 to over one million by 1960. And in the same period of time the percentage of Negroes in Chicago rose from two to just under twenty-three.[57] And, as we shall see, a good deal of what happens to IM during his early days in New York is sociohistorically relevant.

Nothing that happens to him in the short eighth chapter, however, is particularly interesting or telling on either the personal or the representative level. The chapter summarizes the first impressions that IM, a southern greenhorn, has of New York: the elevators that rise like rockets and create a sensation in the crotch as though one's private parts have been left below; the "spell of power and mystery" of the metropolis; the impersonality of the city dwellers; the swift alternations of fantasies of success and self-conscious uncertainty. The chapter does sketch a phase of IM's northward rite of passage; but its notations are unremarkable and dispensable. Had one been in an editorial position to do so, it would have been hard not to urge that the chapter be either merged with the equally short chapter 7, thereby making the former's bland contents less conspicuous, or dropped entirely and a brief link-passage supplied at the end of the previous chapter.

In contrast, the ninth chapter of *Invisible Man* crackles with fresh invention and vivid, suggestive notation. The chapter is built on two splendidly realized minor characters. One of them is the blues-singing cartman, a black from the South who is in the city but does not have the city in him. The scene in which he meets the fast-talking cartman is the first of a number of incidents that evoke memories of the world IM has left behind. The southern memories stimulated in chapter 9 are necessarily folk memories, for the cartman is a composite of black folk motifs. In the first place, the name he calls himself by—Peter Wheatstraw—refers to Peetie Wheatstraw, the blues singer, who in one of his songs called himself "the Devil's Son-in-law," just as Ellison's character calls himself. But the blues singer's real name was William Bunch; the performance name he chose was a traditional Negro folk name, like Jack the Rabbit, Jack the Bear, and High John the Conqueror, all of which are mentioned by the cartman and are part of the

verbal highjinks that include Negro folk expressions, rhymes and recognition rituals ("is you got the *dog?*"), as well as a rendering of the
"Boogie Woogie Blues."

During their conversation, a lot of "stuff" from childhood and
adolescence that IM had known "but long ago shut out of my mind"
stirs within him; a "wave of homesickness" overcomes him, as does
the déjà vu feeling that he and the cartman "had walked this way
before through other mornings, in other places." These reminders,
however, do not shake IM's resolve to slough off his southern ways of
speech now that he is in the North, and in other ways to sever his
roots; "*they're* a hell of a people" (my italics) is his last thought about
the cartman.

But the raison d'être of the cartman scene, unlike that of the yam-
eating scene in chapter 13, is not to stimulate IM's southern memories
and his sense of racial identity. Its principal aesthetic function is found
in the contrast between the cartman and the other character introduced in chapter 9, Mr. Emerson's son, whose office IM visits in the
chapter's second half. The contrast is a less intense and complex (because the two characters do not interact with each other) and more
comic restatement of the Trueblood-Norton contrast in chapter 2.
Trueblood and the cartman are both earthy, uneducated southern
blacks steeped in the same predominantly oral culture. Both colorfully
speaking blues singers have a strong, culturally derived sense of identity; and both are shown to have a healthy extroverted sexuality—
Trueblood's reveries about his sweet nights in Mobile with Margaret
are paralleled by the cartman's lusty singing about his "baby," who is
not good-looking but is a great lover, and whom he loves (just as
Trueblood loves his family) "*better than I do myself.*"

In contrast, Mr. Norton and Mr. Emerson's son, both educated,
wealthy, and fair-haired, are establishment northern liberals in the
mainstream of the American patrician tradition. While Mr. Norton
cites Ralph Waldo Emerson, young Emerson at one point is heard to
mutter something about "nostalgia for Harvard yard." Unlike their
black opposites, however, both white men have a weak sense of identity ("who has any identity any more anyway?" Emerson defensively

observes). Indeed, the fragility of their sense of self is the reason both men confide in IM the first time they meet him. In each case the question of identity is further complicated (and destabilized) by a sexual underside that is connected with Negroes. As we have seen, Norton's philanthropic activities on behalf of southern blacks are contaminated by his incestuous feelings toward his daughter. Similarly, Emerson's seemingly altruistic attempt to help IM is contaminated not only by his neurotic self-concern but also by his homosexual tastes. "With us it's still Jim and Huck Finn," he tells IM at one point, citing what Leslie Fiedler, in his famous 1948 *Partisan Review* essay, "Come Back to the Raft Ag'in, Huck Honey!" (which it is hard to imagine Ralph Ellison not having read), identifies as a prime example of the American archetype of the mutual homoerotic love of a white man and a dark other.[58]

It is neatly suggested in the text that the malaise of Mr. Emerson's son is rooted in his relationship to his patriarchal father (Mr. Norton's malaise is similarly rooted in a parent-child relationship). "No one speaks *to* him," says young Emerson as he "mashes his cigarette into the tray with shaking fingers." "*He* does the speaking." In another place he exclaims that "Mr. Emerson is my father . . . though I would have preferred it otherwise"; and of President Bledsoe he observes, "He's like my [father]. He ought to be horsewhipped!" In short, "I'm still his prisoner." Not for nothing is the neurotic son shown to be reading Freud's *Totem and Taboo* when IM enters his office. The subtitle of Freud's work is *Some Points of Agreement between the Mental Lives of Savages and Neurotics;* its climax is a psychoanalytic reconstruction of the origin of its dual subject in the "great event with which civilization began and which, since it occurred, has not allowed mankind a moment's rest"—the killing of the primal father by his sons.[59]

As the droll scene between IM and young Emerson develops, the latter makes a play for the former. The comedy is generated by the contrast between the innocent incomprehension of IM and the various moves, ranging from the stereotypical to the flamboyant, in Emerson's homosexual pass. They are not long into their conversation when

Emerson, who moves "with a long hip-swinging stride," is commenting on the athletic build of IM. Soon after, IM is asked if he has ever been to the Calamus Club. "Calamus" being the name of the section of Whitman's *Leaves of Grass* containing his poems of manly love, one can hardly doubt what is behind the question. Nor does one miss the double meaning in Emerson's reference to the need to "throw off the mask of custom and manners that insulate man from man, and converse in *naked* honesty and frankness" (my italics). Soon after this, he touches IM's knee "lightly and quickly." Then follows the reference to *Huckleberry Finn*, which is way over IM's head ("Why did he keep talking about that kid's story?"). Finally, after an invitation to join him and friends at the Calamus is declined, comes young Emerson's inspired final play: "Perhaps you'd like to be my valet?"

While the two principal scenes that make up chapter 9 can be savored for their own sakes, the reflective reader of *Invisible Man* will want at some point to think about the aesthetic function of the chapter's restatement of the Trueblood-Norton contrast. Is there a significant variation within the similarity that makes for aesthetic discourse? Or is the patterning simply a repetition, and as such more decorative than illuminating? One way of addressing the question would be to ask what would be missing from *Invisible Man* if chapter 9 were expunged from its text and whether the rest of the novel would be made significantly different by its absence. Whatever one decided, it would have to be admitted that, on the level of thematic motifs, one could not do without the revelation (at the end of the scene with young Emerson) of the contents of Bledsoe's letters to the important northern friends of the college. What the circumloquacious epistolary discourse of Bledsoe reduces to is the same brutally simple sentence that provided the punch line in the dream of IM that closes chapter 1: "Keep This Nigger-Boy Running."

As soon as he finishes reading the letter, IM experiences a sense of déjà vu for the second time in the chapter. But this one is very different from the warm feeling evoked by the cartman's patter. "I could not believe it," IM says of the letter, "yet I had a feeling that it all had happened before." We are not told what the source of this feeling is, but one can reasonably infer that what pings in IM's mind is the dream described at the end of chapter 1. And it is not farfetched to reflect, as one commentator has done, that "in a way, it *has* happened before; for Bledsoe's act of victimization (the beating of Negro by Negro) is analogous to the punishment [IM] received in the prize-ring at the hands of the largest of the other Negro boys."[60]

When he leaves Emerson's office, IM takes a bus and finds himself sitting behind a man whistling a song, an "old forgotten jingle about a bare-rumped robin." It is clear that the song—a mock funeral dirge lamenting the picking clean of "poor Robin"—makes a ruefully ironic comment on Bledsoe's cruel deception. But for readers of *Invisible Man* who find themselves wondering, as IM himself does, about the larger meaning of the song, the following comments from a 1962 essay by Ellison will be interesting—not least of all because they provide another example of the author's after-the-fact tendency to accentuate the positive, both in his novel and in black racial experience in the United States:

> Back in the thirties members of the old Blue Devils Orchestra celebrated a certain robin by playing a lugubrious little tune called "They Picked Poor Robin." It was a jazz community joke, musically an extended "signifying riff" or melodic naming of a recurring human situation, and was played to satirize some betrayal of faith or loss of love observed from the bandstand. Sometimes it was played as the purple-fezzed musicians returned from the burial of an Elk. . . .
> Poor robin was picked again and again and his pluckers were ever unnamed and mysterious. Yet the tune was inevitably productive of laughter—even when we ourselves were its object. For each of us recognized that his fate was somehow our own. Our defeats and failures—even our final defeat by death—were loaded upon his back and given ironic significance and thus made more bearable.[61]

Chapter 10 of *Invisible Man*, the paint factory episode, is divided into three parts, of which the first is the most important. Indeed, the paint-mixing scene is the most artistically satisfying and richly suggestive fusion of the novel's literal and symbolic levels. While everything that happens is plausible and no part of the narrative surface seems manipulated or distorted, the whole scene resonates with suggestiveness. And while one might wonder how essential to *Invisible Man*, and how ultimately telling, is the cartman-Emerson contrast in chapter 9, there can be no doubt about the thematic importance of the paint-mixing scene.

Nothing that happens at the narrative level in the scene will surprise any college student who has held a summer job in a factory. An ignorant, self-important, and loud-talking foreman—a white man named Kimbro—assigns IM a mechanical, repetitive task, giving neither an explanation of its purpose nor proper instructions for its performance. Ten drops of a dead-black liquid are to be measured into "every single sonofabitching bucket" of a rush shipment of white paint. IM has no idea why the black liquid makes the paint appear whiter. Nor does he know from which tank to get a refill of the liquid. He guesses wrong and begins to panic when he realizes that drops of the new liquid make the paint less white and glossy and give it a gray tinge. Kimbro blows his top when he discovers that the black liquid IM is using is concentrated remover, and storms off without saying what should be done with the spoiled paint. IM, "seized by an angry impulse," stirs ten drops of the correct liquid into each bucket, and then, for better or worse, places them with the unspoiled paint awaiting shipment. When Kimbro next comes round, he checks the work IM has been doing since his mistake was corrected and declares the correctly treated paint to be "the way it oughta be." IM listens "with a sense of unbelief"; for when he examines the sample that the foreman had scrutinized, he finds that "a gray tinge glowed through the whiteness, and Kimbro had failed to detect it."

One of the first things the attentive reader begins to notice about this scene are the suggestions that the paint factory—so big "it looks like a small city"—represents America, more particularly, white American society. In the chapter's opening paragraph, the first thing IM sees as he approaches the factory is a huge electric sign announcing the company motto: Keep America Pure with Liberty Paints. The company trademark—a screaming eagle—is the same as the insignia of the United States of America, and much of the paint produced is made for the federal government. For example, the batch of the top-of-the-line Optic White on which IM is set to work is headed for a national monument. It is, says Kimbro, a paint that will "cover just about anything"; it is "as white as George Washington's Sunday-go-to-meetin' wig and as sound as the all-mighty dollar!"

Such hard-to-miss signals are only the beginning. According to the company's motto, America is not just to be kept freshly painted by Liberty Paints, but is to be kept pure—a word with distinct metaphorical overtones, as in phrases like "racial purity" and "moral purity." The color of purity, of course, is white, as in the expression "pure as the driven snow." It would seem, however, that the whiteness of American purity is intensified by the admixture of a strictly controlled amount of black—ten drops per bucket. At this point, one might well recall that the black population of the United States is ten percent of the total. And the same number, of course, recalls the addition of the ten black boys to the white men's smoker in chapter 1 and retrospectively adds to the suggestiveness of that scene. (For one thing, it brings more into focus the tellingness of the small American flag tatooed on the belly of the nude blond dancer.)

Once one is teased into reflection by details like these, the symbolic richness of the paint-mixing scene begins to exfoliate. What, one might wonder, does the use of black drops to intensify the whiteness of white paint mean on the symbolic level? Are the black drops those American Negroes who emulate white values and aspirations, thereby endorsing and strengthening the white-American way? One example of such blacks, of course, would be those who follow the precepts of Booker T. Washington. It is not for nothing that as he stirs the black drops into the white paint IM wonders whether it is the same paint used on the buildings of the college. One might further reflect that his southern black college was dependent on the financial support of whites from the industrialized North, among them Mr. Norton, who, as we have seen, makes himself feel morally and spiritually whiter (purer) through his philanthropic patronage of Negroes and his sentimental identification with their destiny.

But the black drops could also be thought to suggest those Negroes who have been either manipulated into playing a role in the maintenance and intensification of the whiteness of white society (it is the role that the rednecks who treat Trueblood well after his disgrace try to impose on him) or co-opted into believing what in chapter 3 the vet at the Golden Day calls "that great false wisdom taught slaves and pragmatists alike, that white is right." Examples of the latter were noted by de Tocqueville in the nineteenth century.

> The Negro makes a thousand fruitless efforts to insinuate himself among men who repulse him; he conforms to the tastes of his oppressors, adopts their opinions, and hopes by imitating them to form a part of their community. Having been told from infancy that his race is naturally inferior to that of the whites, he assents to the proposition and is ashamed of his own nature. In each of his features he discovers a trace of slavery, and if it were in his power, he would willingly rid himself of everything that makes him what he is.[62]

A specific example of co-option from within in *Invisible Man* would be Lucius Brockway (who appears later on in chapter 10), an Uncle Tom figure who was once given a bonus by the company owner for his role in fabricating the slogan, If It's Optic White, It's the Right White.

But the slogan about Optic White being the right white and the fact that ultimately Kimbro and IM see the same color differently suggests that, at one level, the paint, or at least the uses to which it is put, is an (optical) illusion. That some of the special white paint is going to Washington to cover a national monument hints at a national whitewash designed to absorb black Americans into a sanitized history of American life—to cover the black truth with a glossy white mythology, including screaming eagles, George Washington at prayer, and the ideal of material affluence represented by the almighty dollar. One recalls both the whitewashed stones in the opening paragraph of chapter 5, that were said to have "cryptic messages" for the black students at the college, and Lucius Brockway's remark about the paint he helped make being "so white you can paint a chunka coal and you'd have to crack it open with a sledge hammer to prove it wasn't white clear through." Of course, one powerful reason for the whites' exclusion of blacks from a "pure" American history would be to provide an implicit justification for their exclusion from the economic and other opportunities of the American way of life. That is what is intimated by IM's hearing in the Optic White slogan an echo of the childhood jingle which begins "If you're white, you're right" and which is elaborated in the blues song used as an epigraph for this chapter.

There are two other incidents near the end of the paint-mixing scene that also have a symbolic overlay, though their suggestiveness is not as rich or sharply focused. When left on his own without prior instruction, IM fills his empty beaker from the wrong tank; as a result he starts putting drops of concentrated remover into the buckets of white paint, which gives the paint not an enhanced whiteness but a gray tinge. One might observe that what was previously invisible has been rendered visible, and further reflect that on a symbolic level what is being suggested is that careful calculation and expert manipulation are needed to make the American whitewash of its black component effective; and that when left on their own or when imperfectly controlled, blacks will begin to make their presence visible in America. Something rather less univocal is suggested by the final incident in the scene: Kimbro's failure to notice in the correctly treated paint a gray tinge that IM is (now?) able to see. One of the two must be experiencing a kind of optical illusion; no matter who, it is hard to miss the point that the American reality looks different to blacks than it does to whites. One might further reflect that the perceptual discrepancy suggests that for white Americans, blacks are invisible—as the narrator IM, in the first paragraph of the novel's prologue, and the crazy vet at the Golden Day had both insisted, and as events and recognitions later in *Invisible Man* will underline.

After IM is sent packing by Kimbro, he is reassigned to Lucius Brockway; since he has to return to the factory locker room in order to get his lunch, he is exposed to a union meeting taking place there. This middle section of chapter 10 also has something superadded to the realistic level; but in this case it is not a symbolic overlay but a sociohistorical relevance. These scenes suggest, in a necessarily sketchy way, some of the central characteristics of black experience in the industrialized North during the early twentieth century. The indispensable Lucius Brockway, for example, who works obscurely in his underground room preparing the basic materials without which "Liberty Paints wouldn't be worth a plugged nickel," may be taken to represent the underpaid and uneducated substratum of black labor on which American industry is built. As Brockway recalls conversations with Mr. Sparland, the owner of the factory, it becomes clear that their relationship is one of paternalistic exploitation. That Brockway is at ease in this old dispensation, and comfortable in his Uncle Tom role, is clear from his violently antiunion feelings. He is also apprehensive about the younger blacks the company has employed, who are presumably among those who had continued to migrate from the South after World War I to find jobs in northern industries.

These younger blacks were unfamiliar with unions and their emerging functions and therefore open to exploitation by the white industrialists, who used them as scab laborers in attempting to break union power. "You new [black] guys don't know the scene," as the office boy explains to IM at the beginning of chapter 10; "Just like the union says, it's the wise guys in the office [i.e., management]. They're the ones who make scabs out of you." In principle, American unions were opposed to racial prejudice; but in practice, like the union group in the locker room, they were far from color-blind. In the scene in which IM inadvertently enters a union meeting, he is greeted with suspicion, treated in a discriminatory way, and patronized ("we don't want to forget that workers like him aren't so highly developed as some of us who've been in the labor movement for a long time"). IM is deeply offended by the treatment he receives at the meeting, and the reader can fully understand the intensity of his reaction only if he has some awareness of the generic aspect of the episode.

The last part of chapter 10, however, makes it artistically clear that the union treatment of IM and the management's treatment of both Brockway and its black scabs are finally to be seen as two more examples of the "Keep This Nigger-Boy Running" syndrome. Violence erupts during the scene as IM and Brockway fight and come close to killing each other. Why are they fighting? The important reason is found not in the content of chapter 10 but in the formal motifs of *Invisible Man*. Ultimately, IM and Brockway are fighting for the same reason that the ten black youths batter each other in the ring in chapter 1, that two black men fight nearly to the death on a Harlem sidewalk in chapter 17, and that a race riot erupts in Harlem in chapter 25. In each case, in one way or another, the violence is attributable either to the manipulation of blacks by representatives of white America or to the imposition of unbearable psychological pressure by the white majority on the black ten percent.

The scene and the chapter end with an explosion—a "wet blast of black emptiness that was somehow a bath of whiteness"—that provides a pyrotechnical envoi to the black-white variations of chapter 10. IM is injured in the explosion and sent to the factory hospital, where the next chapter of *Invisible Man* is set. This chapter continues the story of the introduction of a young southern black to the industrial north, but the subject is artistically rendered in a very different way.

Chapter 11 is extremely interesting to the student of *Invisible Man* because it exists in two quite different versions. The earlier, 17,500-word version was included in the manuscript of *Invisible Man* that Ellison sent to his publishers. It was subsequently dropped from the text and, some years later, in 1963, was published on its own in an anthology of new writing by American Negroes under the title "Out of the Hospital and under the Bar."[63] The other version is the 5,600-word chapter that appears in the published text of the novel. Ellison has more than once explained how the shorter version came to be substituted for the longer one. In 1963 he wrote that "Out of the Hospital" (as I shall call the earlier version) had been drafted "during those expansive days of composition before the necessities of publication became a reality. . . . I was quite sorry that considerations of space made it necessary that I reconceive the development." And in 1977 an interviewer was told: "Well, the book was long and they wanted cuts, and I found a better way than just cutting was to restructure. So, instead of that particular handling of the narrative sequence I just took it out. I think it would have probably worked better in."[64] Despite Ellison's retrospective explanations, however, it is hard to believe that quantitative considerations were the only, or even the most important, reasons for dropping "Out of the Hospital." The most important difference between the two versions is not in length but in the presentation technique—in the way experience is represented. For this reason, a comparison of the two versions offers a valuable insight into the aesthetic calculations and authorial choices that went into the making of *Invisible Man*.

"Out of the Hospital" is written in the realistic-naturalistic mode of many of the chapters of *Invisible Man* (particularly those in its second half) and, like them, contains a degree of symbolic and/or sociohistorical relevance, which has been worked into the narrative material. "Out of the Hospital" opens with IM awakening to find himself encased in some kind of hospital apparatus, being gazed at by an older black woman with "work-swollen fingers" who is one of the hospital's custodial staff. For unaccountable reasons, IM, who is revealed to be suffering from memory loss, has the feeling that he has known this woman for a long time, and he finds her voice strangely familiar. She wonders "why these white folks got you in this iron straight-jacket?" and on realizing that he is a "down-home boy" from the South, decides that what he needs is some proper food. All that she can come up with at short notice is a pork sandwich, which IM finds "delicious;

strange and yet familiar in my mouth." He tells the old woman, whose name is Mary Rambo, that he wants to get out of the hospital, and she agrees to help him escape when she returns the following day.

In the meantime, IM manages to free one of his arms from the machine that contains him. Despite his apprehension, this is noticed neither by a nurse, who seems in a romantic daydream, nor by two physicians who do not really seem to see him at all. IM fills with silent rage as he grasps the paradox that "I really was no freer than before— simply because *they* refused to acknowledge my freedom. . . . They had locked me in their eyes like a tadpole in a jug. . . . Nobody bothered to notice the bare arm, the clenched fist." When Mary returns she brings "a little home remedy, something I got from my mama," that has the consistency of chewing tobacco and scorches his throat, but which does seem mysteriously to restore his strength. This, and a prayer to the Lord to "give me the strength of Jack-the-Bear," enables IM to break out of the machine. As he leaves the hospital, he thinks of Lincoln's freeing of the slaves, and the ensuing pursuit of the naked young man trying to escape from the hospital inevitably calls to mind antebellum pursuits of escaped slaves. A series of bizarre escapades brings IM into face-to-face contact with a corpse; and into a dark basement storage room ("Talking about a nigger in a wood pile! Whew!" exclaims one of his pursuers) and a coal bin under a bar. He reaches street level through a manhole cover and is assisted by several friendly, drunken black men, who assume he is naked owing to his having to leave an amorous rendezvous unexpectedly. "Dig this here game stud! . . . Well help him then, and let him go. I once had to grab me an armful of window myself." Clothed, back on the street, and heading for Mary's place, IM meets an old blind man who becomes important for him in the "frantic urgency" of his "need to know something definite about myself." Why is the blind man's face so familiar, IM wonders; why does he sound "like someone I know? . . . Had I dreamed him?" As the blind man walks away, IM yells after him and finds himself calling the man by his grandfather's name and realizing that his face had resembled that of his grandfather. As a result of this recognition, IM's memory finally begins to return. In the closing sentence of "Out of the Hospital," he resolves to get to Mary's and hole up there until his memory fully returns.

What this brief summary cannot convey is a sense of the long-windedness and forced quality of the 17,500 words of "Out of the Hospital," which does not have the freshness or the resonance of the principal earlier chapters of *Invisible Man*. For all its bizarre incidents, the episode quite lacks the exhilarating one-damn-thing-after-another-sheer-happening comic quality of the Golden Day chapter. Moreover, the symbolic incidents are much too heavy-handed and much too univocal in meaning—they thud rather than ping. "Out of the Hospital" does, however, flesh out the character of Mary Rambo, who (as we shall see) figures in the following chapters of *Invisible Man*. Ellison himself has made this point, observing that "she deserved more space in the novel, and would, I think, have made it a better book."[65] But the thematic concern with cultural identity and with roots—all too obviously advertised by the pork sandwich, the folk medicine, and that déjà vu sense of having known both Mary and the blind man—is also a principal subject of chapters 12 through 22. If "Out of the Hospital" had been allowed to precede these chapters, it would have made appreciable parts of them rather redundant. It would have meant doing something twice in the same way—repetition with insufficient variation.

The second and final version of chapter 11 is an enormous improvement. It does not employ the extensive presentational technique of realistic narrative with symbolic and/or sociohistorical overlay. It instead uses intense expressionism whereby the realistic surface is distorted so that the truth of the dynamics of black-white interaction and the recontact with roots is felt. While the teasing-into-thought symbolism of the black drops in white paint in chapter 10 is a superb aid to reflection, chapter 11, not unlike the reefer dream in the prologue or the castration nightmare at the end of chapter 25, is an off-the-beat node, in which the tormented consciousness of IM is represented through hallucination-like distortions. Because the mode of presentation is expressive, it does not matter whether the things described in chapter 11 really took place. Ellison has explained that he employed an expressionistic style in parts of his novel in order to "try to express both [IM's] state of consciousness and the state of society."[66] Chapter 11 attempts to convey in one expressive image both a sense of IM's psychological turmoil and an epitome of what happens to blacks in white America, more particularly, of what happens to black identity in the industrialized North.

The hospital machine to which IM is attached is a synechdoche for the *E pluribus unum* melting pot into which the vet had predicted IM would fall once he reached the North. The machine seems designed, if not to destroy the sense of racial identity of American blacks, at least to neutralize it and render it powerless. This is suggested during an astonishing conversation—a potent mixture of the mordantly comic and the horrifying—that the doctors have as they stand over IM. They casually discuss the ramifications of a prefrontal lobotomy, which would result in a complete personality change, but would leave the patient physically and neurally whole; the importance of society suffering "no traumata" on his account; the option of castration; and so on. As the doctors decide what treatment to give, IM's consciousness begins to fill with vivid, sharply etched memories of his southern past, which are quite unlike the clumsy signposts of "Out of the Hospital" and which do not duplicate similar material in later chapters because the intensive, elliptical mode of presentation is different. Into IM's consciousness flash memories of wading in a brook before breakfast, chewing sugar cane, a grandmother's mock spiritual, and the children's rhyme about Miss Margaret (the activity referred to in the bowdlerized quoted stanza, incidentally, is not that of boiling water but that of urinating). Later, after electric shock therapy, other early memories are stimulated. When a sign is held before IM asking who his mother was, his thought is that he does not want to play the dozens—a verbal game of ritual insult involving an exchange of flamboyant slurs on the opponent's immediate family. And when the written questions being used to stimulate his memory mention common Negro folk motifs, IM remembers a rhyme about Buckeye the Rabbit that "as children we danced and sang barefoot in the dusty streets."

When IM is freed from the machine—the last item to be detached is an umbilical-like cord "attached to the stomach node"—chapter 11 quickly modulates from expressionism to realism. IM's memory seems restored by the treatment he has received, but the larger question of his identity remains unanswered. Before his release from the machine, IM had wondered whether the discovery of his identity was connected with the question of how to escape from the machine. "Perhaps," he had thought, "the two things are involved with each other. When I discover who I am, I'll be free." We shall have to see whether in later chapters of the novel this in fact turns out to be the case. For the moment, however, it is made clear at the end of chapter 11 that, in the figurative sense, IM is still not free of the white machine. He feels inauthentic, "in the grip of some alien personality lodged deep within me. . . . It was as though I were acting out a scene from some crazy movie." That is to say, he is still what the vet had earlier called him, "a walking zombie," who can certainly feel the effects of, but is as yet unable to understand, the brutally simple facts of American life.

7

CHAPTERS 12–22

Some like high-yellows but give me my black an' brown
I said some like high-yellows but give me my black an' brown
'Cause the black will stick by you when the yellow turns you down.
                                        Trixie Smith, "Trixie's Blues"

One intermittently voiced criticism of *Invisible Man* is that there is a comparative falling off in quality in its second half. On the face of it, there does seem to be evidence to warrant this complaint. From chapter 12 at least until its final three chapters, the medium of presentation tends to be more exclusively realistic, with less symbolic and expressive intensity. And, as the story of the character IM approaches the time in which the narrator IM is telling it, episodes and situations are in other ways more extensively and univocally rendered than were those in the earlier parts of the novel. Several chapters and a great many pages, for example, are devoted to IM's involvement with the Brotherhood (i.e., the Communist party), whereas in the first half of the novel one or two condensed and richly suggestive chapters chronicle significant passages in his development—his adolescent years in the southern town where the battle royal takes place, his three years at the Negro college, the time spent getting settled in New York, his exposure to industrial capitalism as a scab laborer. Saul Bellow is not alone in regarding IM's experiences in the Communist party as less "original in conception" than other parts of the book.[67]

Moreover, the characters in the second half are less striking and less richly rendered than those in the first. Of the supporting players who make their appearance after the factory hospital chapter, only one—the black nationalist Ras—is as sharply and memorably rendered as were Trueblood, Bledsoe, Mr. Emerson's son, Lucius Brockway, or even the blues-singing cartman. And the characterization of Jack, the most important figure in IM's life during these later chapters, is conspicuously thin and rises only a little, if at all, above the level of caricature: he was "a short insignificant-looking bushy-eyebrowed man" (chap. 13); "he was like a toy bull terrier" (chap. 16); he was "a little bantam rooster of a man" (chap. 22). When Jack's glass eye pops out in chapter 22 and rolls around the table as he explains that "I lost my eye in the line of duty" (the double meaning is patent), the reader should not really be surprised, for the incident is an epitome, rather than the obverse, of the level at which Jack is characterized.

In addition, some have commented that for all the varied incidents and all the trouble taken with the artistic elaboration of its informing themes, the novel is essentially static. Marcus Klein, for example, argued that its "great fault is that its end *is* its beginning" and that for all its "furious picaresque . . . the novel has no real progress except that at each stage it clarifies and reinforces the hero's dilemma." From this point of view, the very power of the opening chapters of *Invisible Man* becomes an aesthetic miscalculation; for Klein, the battle royal "is an extraordinarily compressed piece of work, and its one fault is that it is both more intensely maintained and more exhaustive than anything else in the novel, and so the hero's adventures hereafter become more or less adequate echoes of it."[68]

On the descriptive level, it is not easy to disagree with some of these observations; but the judgmental level is a different matter. I should myself prefer to accentuate the many positives in chapters 12 through 22, by saying that what occurs in this long section of the novel is not so much (if at all) a falling off as a change in tempo and beat, to which the reader must adjust. Until the race riot in chapter 25 there is no single node in the second half of *Invisible Man* equal to the battle royal, or Trueblood's story, or the factory hospital chapter. But there are a number of smaller-scale scenes, with some excellent cameo parts, that are, in their own more univocally realistic mode, as crackling and engaging as the major set pieces earlier in the novel, to which they are linked by a variety of repeated motifs. There is the party at the Chthonian in chapter 14, where IM meets Emma and is embarrassed by the drunken honkie who asks him to sing; the eviction scene in chapter 13, at which IM makes an impromptu speech; the speech in the sports arena in chapter 16; the seduction scene in chapter 19; Tod Clifton's funeral in chapter 21; and in chapter 17 the fight scene on a Harlem street under the Checks-Cashed-Here sign, a scene dominated by the anguished voice of Ras—the rough staccato eloquence of his West Indian accent leaps from the page. Similarly, there is a cumulative thematic density to these chapters, in which concerns introduced earlier in the novel are elaborated in nonrepetitive ways, while other concerns are developed for the first time. Among the most important of these are the sexual level of black-white relations; the importance of roots, and the relationship of the southern past to the northern present for American blacks in general and for IM in particular; and the question of black leadership.

SEXUALITY

Houston Baker has called black male sexuality "one of the dominant themes" of *Invisible Man* and has identified the "black male phallus as a dominant symbol in much of the ritual interaction" of the novel.[69] I should not go nearly so far as this myself; but one can hardly deny that the novel contains a good deal of telling notation of the socio-sexual aspect of black-white relations, and that in aggregate these notations amount to a thematization of the subject. But this is only to be expected in a novel that takes black-white relations in the United States as one of its central subjects. As Ellison has acutely observed:

> Anyone writing from the Negro American point of view with any sort of thoroughness would certainly have had to write about the potential meaning and the effects of the relationship between black women and white men and black men and white women, because this became an essence; and a great part of the society was controlled by the taboos built around the fear of the white woman and the black man getting together. Great political power and, to some extent, great military ardor were brewed from this socio-sexual polarization. And so, any novelist who is going to write from the Negro background would certainly have to deal with these particular aspects of our society. They're unpleasant; and yet, it is in the unpleasant, in that which is charged with emotion, with fears, with irrationality, that we find great potential for transforming attitudes. So I tried to face them with a certain forthrightness, to treat them ironically, because they are really destructive in a kind of comic and absurd way.[70]

Mention has already been made of a number of telling sociosexual notations in the first half of the novel: the black woman who speaks with such ambivalent feelings about her white master-lover in the reefer-vision of the prologue; the nude blond dancer watched by the white big shots and the ten black youths at the smoker in chapter 1; Trueblood's dream in chapter 2 and Mr. Norton's destabilizing fascination with its incestuous culmination; the broadly comic exchanges in the bedroom of the Golden Day; and the contrast in chapter 9 between the cartman's lusty singing about his love for his ugly, but sexually fulfilling, woman and the homosexual pass made by Mr. Emerson's son. There are an equal number of important notations in the second half of the novel grounded in the experiences of IM himself.

A good place to begin is the moment when IM meets Emma in the doorway of her posh apartment at the Chthonian. As he crosses the threshold, Emma does not step back and IM finds himself "pressing tensely against her perfumed softness, seeing her smile as though there were only she and I." Having passed her, IM reports that he was "disturbed not so much by the close contact, as by the sense that I had somehow been through it all before. I couldn't decide if it were from watching some similar scene in the movies, from books I'd read, or from some recurrent but deeply buried dream." The reader is clearly meant to be intrigued by IM's sense of déjà vu, and to wonder about its cause. One knows almost nothing about his taste in movies or his reading habits, but one does know a good deal about significant moments in his postpuberty life that may have provided the experiential basis for either the uncanny feeling itself or the buried dream that has possibly triggered it. In fact, there are no fewer than three earlier moments in the text that are retrospectively illuminated when IM presses close against Emma and senses that he has somehow "been through it all before."

Since this feeling began when he entered the Chthonian, a privileged white enclave, as the guest of a group of Caucasian males, we may be reminded of the white man's smoker and the magnificent nude blonde, the sight of whom stimulated intense and ambivalent feelings in IM, who felt the simultaneous urge "to caress her and destroy her, to love her and murder her, to hide from her, and yet to stroke" the area below the tattooed American flag. One also recalls IM's "shudder of nameless horror" in the Golden Day in chapter 2, when he is pressed up against Mr. Norton: "I had never been so close to a white person before. In a panic I struggled to get away. . . . He was like a formless white death." Finally, one remembers the similarly horror-struck moment in the subway in chapter 7, when IM finds himself crushed against a huge white woman and feels "the rubbery softness of her flesh against the length of my body," while he stares at the "large mole that arose out of the oily whiteness of her skin like a black mountain sweeping out of a rain-wet plain."

A few minutes after meeting Emma, IM overhears her cynical remark about his perhaps not being black enough for the Brotherhood's purposes. His immediate response is aggressively sexual: "I'd like to show her how black I really am." But he is docile enough shortly after, when Emma reaches into the bosom of her taffeta gown to remove the paper containing his new Brotherhood name. Shortly after that, Emma asks him to dance, thereby fulfilling the whispered prediction of the vet on the bus going north in chapter 7: in New York "you might even dance with a white girl!"

As they dance, Emma admires IM's verbal repartee and suggests that he "come up and fence with [her] some afternoon" (chap. 23). She is not the only white woman in the novel to make sexual overtures to him. The unnamed woman in chapter 19, who attends his lectures on the woman question but confuses "the class struggle with the ass struggle," is the first to get him into bed. His seduction by her is one of the drollest scenes in the novel. The comedy is controlled by the manipulation of two sexual stereotypes. One is the socially elevated white woman sexually attracted to the black male. Not for nothing does IM's mind whirl during this scene "with forgotten stories of male servants summoned to wash the mistress's back; chauffeurs sharing the masters' wives; Pullman porters invited into the drawing room of rich wives headed for Reno." The complementary stereotype, of course, is that of the primitive sexual potency of the black male stud. "Yes, primitive," the seductress tells IM as she moves closer to him on the couch. "No one has told you, Brother, that at times you have tom-toms beating in your voice?"

While this scene is scored for comedy, it nonetheless dramatizes a serious aspect of the complex and dehumanizing dynamics of black-white interaction. As Ellison explained in an essay written in 1945, the year he began work on *Invisible Man:* One of the psychological attitudes imposed on Negro life by whites led to a misjudgment of Negro passion, which whites observed from the point of view of "the turgidity of their own frustrated yearning for emotional warmth, their capacity for sensation having been constricted by the impersonal mechanized relationships typical of bourgeois society. The Negro is idealized into a symbol of sensation, of unhampered social and sexual relationships."[71] This under-the-surface dynamic explains a peculiarity that IM notes but cannot "fathom." In speaking to downtown audiences on the woman question, he observes that his female auditors seemed "to expect some unnamed something whenever I appeared. . . . From the moment they turned their eyes upon me they seemed to undergo a strange unburdening. . . . I didn't get it. And my guilt was aroused. . . . Something seemed to occur that was hidden from my own consciousness" (chap. 19). As we shall see, by the second seduction scene in *Invisible Man,* the one in chapter 24, IM the character has learned a good deal about this sociosexual syndrome, which he then encounters in the rawer and more debased form of the drunken Sybil begging her "black brute" to rape her: "Who's taking revenge on whom?" he wonders. "But why be surprised, when that's what they hear all their lives. When it's made into a great power and they're taught to worship all types of power? With all the warnings against it, some are bound to want to try it out for themselves."

But of course this desire is a two-way street, or so Ras implies in chapter 17 when he asks IM if he has joined the predominantly white Brotherhood because they "give you them stinking women." In Ras's anguished analysis, the white man betrays and subjugates the black man by putting white strumpets in front of him and telling him "his freedom lie between her skinny legs," while keeping "the good white women . . . locked up," by telling them that "the black mahn is a rapist." Ras, the black nationalist, is a mentally disturbed rabble-rouser and would-be demagogue, who "goes wild when he sees black people and white people together" in any situation, and whose followers—as someone hyperbolically puts it—"would attack and denounce the white meat of a roasted chicken" (chap. 17). But his intuitive analysis of black-white sexual dynamics cannot be dismissed out of hand. It might, after all, be said to be partially authenticated by the ritual dynamics of the battle royal. And there is no reason not to think that the sexual suggestiveness of Emma's gestures at the Chthonian—not stepping back from the threshold, producing the paper containing IM's new name from the bosom of her gown, inviting him to dance, and uttering innuendoes while her soft closeness triggers a "hot swift focusing" of IM's desire (chap. 23)—are all calculated to draw him into the white net of the Brotherhood. Certainly Ras's analysis is as exaggerated as it is demotically expressed, but it is precisely this distortion that registers the corrosive and dehumanized effects of the black-white sexual syndrome.

ROOTS

At the end of chapter 20, IM comes out of the subway, where he has been struck by the sight of three flashily dressed young men and two black-and-white nuns. As he moves through the crowds along 125th Street, he begins to be aware of—to see for the first time—the colorful people around him: "other men dressed like the boys, and . . . girls in dark exotic-colored stockings, their costumes surreal variations of downtown styles. They'd been there all along," he reflects, but he had missed them because of his blinkered involvement in the Brotherhood. Now he begins to look at them and to notice that hardly one of their faces was "unlike someone I'd known down South." He then begins to notice "a record shop loudspeaker blaring a languid blues" and stops short, suddenly struck by an alarming thought: "Was this all that would be recorded? Was this the only true history of the times, a mood blared by trumpets, trombones, saxophones and drums, a song with turgid, inadequate words?"

In reading this passage, one feels that what the character IM is realizing on the social and political level is, on another level, an adumbration of one of the principal artistic concerns of the narrator IM. One of his informing creative intentions is, unquestionably, to get into his narrative the flow of real life, the complex of sights, sounds, and memories that make up the essential ambience of his life experience and those of his black contemporaries. The severely restricted range of subject matter, emotion, and style that can be accommodated by the blues makes it an inadequate vehicle for the re-creation and communication of the richly varied life he has experienced. He is concerned—both as a Negro and as an artist—that the blues alone not be taken, *faute de mieux*, as a representative history of black experience.

The narrator's concern with achieving representational fullness, with getting a wide spectrum of black life into the novel, is abundantly instanced in the chapters we are examining. For example, chapter 13 describes the sidewalk clutter of objects belonging to the elderly couple being evicted which awakens in IM "strange memories" of the South: the " 'knocking bones' used to accompany music at country dances, used in black-face minstrels"; a straightening comb; nuggets of High John the Conqueror, the lucky stone; a whiskey bottle full of rock candy and camphor; a small Ethiopian flag; a faded tintype of Abraham Lincoln; the smiling image of a Hollywood star torn from a magazine; a yellowing newspaper picture of Marcus Garvey; and a number of other items. The previous chapter describes the black types seen in the lobby of Men's House, all of them still caught up in illusions about making it in the white man's world. Chapter 21 describes the crowds on Eighth Avenue and

> the market carts . . . parked hub to hub along the curb, improvised canopies shading the withering fruits and vegetables. I could smell the stench of decaying cabbage. A watermelon huckster stood in the shade beside his truck, holding up a long slice of orange-meated melon, crying his wares with hoarse appeals to nostalgia, memories of childhood, green shade and summer coolness. Oranges, cocoanuts and alligator pears lay in neat piles on little tables. I passed, winding my way through the slowly moving crowd. Stale and wilted flowers, rejected downtown, blazed feverishly on a cart.

And, as a final example, the Harlem storefronts are described at the beginning of chapter 13:

> I walked, my eyes focused into the endless succession of barber shops, beauty parlors, confectioneries, luncheonettes, fish houses, and hog maw joints, walking close to the windows, the snowflakes lacing swift between, simultaneously forming a curtain, a veil, and stripping it aside. A flash of red and gold from a window filled with religious articles caught my eye. And behind the film of frost etching the glass I saw two brashly painted plaster images of Mary and

Jesus surrounded by dream books, love powders, God-Is-Love signs, money-drawing oil and plastic dice. A black statue of a nude Nubian slave grinned out at me from beneath a turban of gold. I passed on to a window decorated with switches of wiry false hair, ointments guaranteed to produce the miracle of whitening black skin. "You too can be truly beautiful," a sign proclaimed. "Win greater happiness with whiter complexion. Be outstanding in your social set."

Descriptions like these do not merely supply *Invisible Man* with local color and a verisimilar base. They also exemplify some of the distortions of personality and of aspiration that are the grotesque result of racial inequality in the United States: the absurd young men at Men's House, for example, who work as messengers and porters while spending most of their income on the clothing fashionable among Wall Street brokers—"Brooks Brothers suits and bowler hats, English umbrellas, black calfskin shoes and yellow gloves" (chap. 12); or the tawdry religious articles next to the plastic dice and the skin-whitening aids in the Harlem storefront. The descriptions also have a social and historical resonance that keeps the reader aware of the representative aspect of IM's passage from the South to Harlem. That jumble of belongings on the street, for example, as IM vaguely senses, is part of the life experience not only of the dispossessed couple but of himself. And the fruit on the Eighth Avenue market carts, the watermelons and alligator pears, caters to a common nostalgic taste, to memories of childhood, and to southern values and pieties that run deep in IM.

This complex of feelings and their importance to individual development are two of the principal subjects of this section of *Invisible Man*. After passing the black storefronts at the beginning of chapter 13, IM comes upon an old man selling hot buttered yams from an odd-looking wagon. The odor of yams brings "a stab of swift nostalgia." This root vegetable evokes memories of home and school—of the southern world that IM had tried to put behind him when he first came to New York. In chapter 8, his final reflection on the blues-singing cartman ("They're [i.e., blacks from the South] a hell of a people") had been followed by his ordering a drugstore breakfast of orange juice, toast, and coffee after coldly disdaining the pork chop, grits, and hot biscuits recommended by the counterman. But when he takes a bite of the sweet hot yam he has bought, IM is overcome by a sense of his regional, racial, and familial past too overpowering to be suppressed. "What a group of people we are," he reflects (as the reader notes the crucial pronominal change from his parting reflection on the cartman); how peculiar that so many of us can feel humiliated simply by being confronted with something we like. The yams, he says, are his birthmark: "I yam what I am."

Just after this spirited acceptance of his roots comes the eviction scene—the dispossession, the uprooting, of the elderly black couple, whose meager belongings prompt in IM a "pang of vague recognition," which in turn leads to a vivid and sharply focused memory of his mother "hanging wash on a cold windy day, so cold that the warm clothes froze even before the vapor thinned and hung stiff on the line, and her hands white and raw in the skirt-swirling wind and her grey head bare to the darkened sky." The memory is one of only a handful of thoughts of his family and home life that IM has during the entire novel, and the only one of his mother. But there are other less personal and more communal memories of the past that also have the power to touch the quick of his being. At Tod Clifton's funeral in Mount Morris Park, for example, as he listens to the husky baritone of an old man's singing of the slave song "There's Many a Thousand Gone," IM recognizes it as "a song from the past, the past of the campus and the still earlier past of home." As he listens, he realizes he is listening to "something within myself" for which the Brotherhood, which had all the scientific answers, had given him no name.

IM's southern roots not only give him a sense of personal and group identity; they also have an ethical and humane dimension. In the novel this dimension is principally represented by Mary Rambo, the good woman who takes IM in when he returns to Harlem from the factory hospital in a weakened condition. In the foreshortened introduction to Mary at the beginning of chapter 12, her leitmotiv is sounded by the person who observes that "Miss Mary always helping somebody." Mary is less a sharply individualized character than a folk figure representative of a maternal black southern goodness. The descriptive touches with which she is sketched all evoke this homey/wholesome quality: the glasses low down on her nose, the slow smile, the worn brown fingers, the good hot soup. Commentators have associated her with Lonnie Johnson's blues song, "She's My Mary," which intones the praise of the good woman who "helped me to carry on" when "this whole world turned me down" and who will "still be my Mary when everything goes wrong." The same commentators might have gone on to note that this is one of the few blues songs in which a woman is celebrated for something other than her sexual or physical attractions. Miss Mary is defined in maternal, not sexual, terms; as such, it is interesting to note, she differs from virtually every other female character in *Invisible Man*. (The one exception is Miss Susie Gresham, the old matron at the college, who is briefly recalled in a single paragraph near the beginning of chapter 5.)

No wonder, then, that IM feels an "old, almost forgotten relief coming over me" when he comes into the care of Mary; that he thinks of her "as a force, a stable, familiar force like something out of my past" (chap. 12); and that just thinking of her makes him feel better. When IM becomes involved in the Brotherhood and begins a fresh cycle of stifling the emotions that are the root of his humanity, his feelings for Mary serve as an index of his condition. In the first fine careless rapture of his identification with the Brotherhood, he accepts the fact that even if he met Mary in the street he would have to pass her by. Later, when he is beginning to feel that he has lost his way in the Brotherhood, he literally loses his way when, returning to his Harlem district after his tour of duty downtown, he finds himself in a strangely familiar block and realizes that he has almost walked to Mary's door. And at the end of the race-riot scene in the last chapter of the novel, when IM has finally realized the full extent of the Brotherhood's cynical manipulation of him and his race, it is to Mary's that he decides he will return.

IM never does reach Mary's, however, and he eventually realizes that he cannot now "return to Mary's or to any part of my old life" (chap. 25). This is an important point and one of a number of signals that *Invisible Man* contains a more complex and ambivalent attitude than is often realized toward roots, toward the southern past, and toward the complex of values Mary embodies. When Mary gives IM a cup of coffee on the morning he leaves her apartment for the last time, she may mean well, but he nonetheless cannot help noticing "an oily opalescent swirl" on the hot metallic surface of the beverage (chap. 15). And while she makes him good hot soup, when she is short of money she also cooks cabbage day after day, the odor of which, unlike that of the yam, brings depressing memories of "the leaner years of my childhood" (chap. 14) and reminds the reader of both the stale cabbage smell in the apartment of the evicted couple in chapter 13 and the stench of decaying cabbage from the Eighth Avenue market carts in chapter 21. There are similarly telling perceptual notations in other chapters. One of them is the olfactory accompaniment of the nostalgic slave song that so moves IM at Clifton's funeral in chapter 21: "the sick sweetish odor" of embalming fluid, "like the smell of some female dogs in season." Another has an unmistakable significance. While the first yam IM bought in chapter 13 had tasted sublime, the second yam was a different story: "an unpleasant taste bloomed in my mouth now as I bit the end of the yam and threw it into the street; it had been frost-bitten." Similarly, while IM's memories of home and childhood can touch the root of piety, they can also be unpleasant and threatening—as in chapter 16 when the smell of carbolic acid prompts a paragraph-long remembrance of a syphilitic who lived alone in a shanty between a railroad yard and a great abandoned hole in the earth and who, when begging for food and disinfectant, would stretch out "a hand from which the fingers had been eaten away."

IM's positive development in the novel is toward individuality via critical self-understanding, and it therefore carries him further and further away from group identity. One of the "many things about people like Mary that I dislike," IM reflects in an important passage at the end of chapter 14, is that "they seldom know where their personalities end and yours begins; they usually think in terms of 'we' while I have always tended to think in terms of 'me'—and that has caused some friction, even with my own family." Even Jack understands this process; while the inference he draws from it is wrong, his diagnosis in chapter 13 of IM's relationship to his familial and folk past has much to recommend it. "Oh, no, brother," he tells IM, "you're mistaken and you're sentimental. You're not like them [the evicted couple]. Perhaps you were but you're not any longer. . . . You have not completely shed that self, that old agrarian self, but it's dead and you will throw it off completely and emerge something new." On the last page of *Invisible Man,* the narrator IM, in referring to himself and his next step, will use exactly the same image of "shaking off the old skin." And the epilogue contains an even stronger endorsement of the words of advice that IM received from the vet as early as chapter 7. "Be your own father, young man. And remember the world is possibility if only you'll discover it." This advice in turn is related to a very important statement concerning the need for blacks to make "ourselves individuals" that (at the end of chapter 16) IM remembers Woodridge making to his literature class back at the college—a statement that relates directly to the question of black political leadership.

LEADERSHIP

In his 1969 speech to the cadets at the United States Military Academy, Ellison recounted that, at the time the novel that was to become *Invisible Man* was germinating in his mind, he was reading Lord Raglan's *The Hero* (selections from which were required reading for West Point plebes):

> I was concerned with the nature of leadership, and thus with the nature of the hero, precisely because during the historical moment when I was working out the concept of *Invisible Man* my people were involved in a terrific quarrel with the federal govermnent over

our not being allowed to participate in the war as combat personnel
in the armed forces on an equal basis, and because we were not
even being allowed to work in the war industries on an equal basis
with other Americans. This quarrel led to my concern with the nature of leadership, to the nature of Negro leadership, from a different and nonliterary direction. I was very much involved with the
question of just why our Negro leadership was never able to enforce
its will. Just what was there about the structure of American society
that prevented Negroes from throwing up effective leaders? Thus it
was no accident that the young man in my book turned out to be
hungry and thirsty to prove to himself that he could be an effective
leader.[72]

This interest in effective leadership is directly reflected in the text
of *Invisible Man*. The portrait of Bledsoe in the early chapters is of a
ruthlessly self-serving black leader; and in chapter 5, as we have seen,
a mythic model for black leadership is provided in Homer A. Barbee's
eulogy of the founder. During IM's stay in her apartment, Mary
Rambo talks constantly about "leadership and responsibility" and
constantly reminds him "that something was expected of me, some act
of leadership, some newsworthy achievement" (chap. 12). And in
chapter 13, as the anger of the crowd watching the eviction grows,
and as an onlooker observes that "all they need is a leader," IM notices
that anger is not their only group emotion; there is also a self-consciousness about the crowd "as though, they, we, were ashamed to
witness the eviction." It is this volatile mixture of anger and shame
that finally ignites his first act of black leadership, his impromptu
speech to the crowd.

As IM comes to realize, the fundamental problem confronting a
potential black leader is the lack of an infrastructure: "We had no
money, no intelligence apparatus, either in government, business or
labor unions; and no communications with our own people except
through unsympathetic newspapers, a few Pullman porters who
brought provincial news from distant cities, and a group of do-
mestics who reported the fairly uninteresting lives of their employers"

(chap. 23). One of the reasons the Brotherhood is attractive to IM is that it is effectively organized, both conceptually and practically. As he reflects at the end of chapter 17: "The organization had given the world a new shape, and me a vital role. We recognized no loose ends, everything could be controlled by our science. Life was all pattern and discipline; and the beauty of discipline is when it works. And it was working very well."

The Brotherhood's criticism of IM's first political speech for them—the one in the Harlem sports arena in chapter 16—is not without point. As the Brotherhood member with the pipe insists, the speech was unsatisfactory because "it was the antithesis of the scientific approach. Ours is a reasonable point of view . . . the audience isn't thinking, it's yelling its head off." The more important criticism, however, is that the speech is also unsatisfactory at the personal and at the leadership-development levels. IM may claim in its peroration that he is being transformed even as he speaks and is becoming "more human," but the claim is specious. The kind of speech IM makes is one he is familiar with from political meetings in the South: "the old down-to-earth, I'm-sick-and-tired-of-the-way-they've-been-treating-us approach." For this reason, any transformation he undergoes is contained within the rabble-rousing rhetorical simplifications of his down-home political culture, and not in the critical self-awareness and unillusioned awareness of the individual's relation to society that is, in *Invisible Man*, the only proper ground for inner development. This speech is sometimes given high marks by commentators because it comes from the heart rather than the head—is emotional rather than scientific, personal rather than political. But it is inauthentically personal, and its emotions are derivative in content and inferior in quality.

No wonder Jack's view of black leadership is so cynical. He may say that the people always generate their leaders, but he believes that leaders are made, not born, and are eventually destroyed by the people, "who chew them up and spit them out" (chap. 14). This view of the nonspontaneous generation of black leaders might seem challenged by the moment in the race-riot scene in chapter 25 when IM,

observing at first hand how two men named Dupre and Scofield organize their neighbors to effective action, is seized with "a fierce sense
of exaltation. They've done it, I thought. They organized it and carried
it through alone; the decision their own and their own action. Capable
of their own action." We shall see, however, that viewed in a larger
context, the home-grown heroics of Dupre and Scofield become much
more problematic, to say the least.

Is Jack, therefore, basically correct in his analysis or does *Invisible
Man* present any constructive suggestions as to what an effective black
leader would be like and from where he would come? In considering
this question one must keep in mind that *Invisible Man* is essentially
a novel of personal development, not of politics. The enabling condition of effective leadership is clearly shown to lie in self-discovery and
the attainment of individuality. This key point is put into the mouth,
not of a political theoretician, but of a college literature teacher called
Woodridge, whose lecture IM recalls at the end of chapter 16. Referring to the last page of Joyce's *Portrait of the Artist as a Young Man*,
he had insisted that Stephen Dedalus's real problem was not "actually
one of creating the uncreated conscience of his race, but of creating
the *uncreated features of his face*. Our task is that of making ourselves
individuals. The conscience of a race is the gift of its individuals who
see, evaluate, record."

The attainment of an authentic identity, however, is not synony-
mous with the actualization of leadership potential—a point that is
implicitly made in the scene describing Tod Clifton's funeral in chapter
21, during which IM makes his last public speech. Compared to the
sports-arena speech, IM's address to the crowd in Mount Morris Park
is truly personal—a sign of his developing humanity and growing understanding of himself and the world. But the speech does not go "the
way I wanted it to go, it wasn't political." IM is "unable to bring in
the political issues" and lead the crowd in the direction of effective
political action in the present. Because of this lack of leadership, the
emotions of the crowd listening to the "old slave-borne words" of
"There's Many a Thousand Gone" are channeled toward the nostalgic
past and the transcendent future and away from the political present.

Light can be shed on the novel's exploration of the subject of black leadership by the unsigned column of "Editorial Comment" that Ellison, then its managing editor, contributed to the *Negro Quarterly* in 1943, at the height of the quarrel between Negro spokesmen and the federal government over black participation in the war effort. In the editorial Ellison identified and severely criticized what he regarded as two pernicious Negro responses to the quarrel. One was that of "unqualified acceptance of the limited opportunity for Negro participation in the conflict." Such an attitude was a vicious form of "uncletomism" that arises from "a lack of any group self-consciousness [and] precludes any confidence in the Negro people's own judgment, or in its potentialities for realizing its own will." The second attitude was one of unqualified rejection of the war, arising out of "a type of Negro nationalism which, in a sense, is admirable." But this view was ultimately rooted in the fatalistic attitude that Negroes could "become conscious of themselves as *Negroes* only in terms of dying." The roots of this attitude were in the folk period before the Negro masses had become politically conscious. But in today's political world "such an attitude is inadequate to deal with its complex problems."[73]

In *Invisible Man,* these two attitudes are represented by Bledsoe and Ras, respectively. The former is "a leader, a 'statesman' who carried our problems to those above us, even unto the White House," much as Booker T. Washington himself had, and who abased himself before whites in public the more effectively to be able to aggrandize himself as a "coal-black daddy" of his race (chap. 5). Ras, on the other hand, is in a way admirable, "wrong but justified, crazy and yet coldly sane," as IM puts it in chapter 25, "but dangerous as well"—in short, a striking foreshadowing of some of the black-power militants of the 1960s.

The failure of these two forms of Negro leadership is tragically underlined in the fate of Tod Clifton, who may be said to represent the potential of black America. Clifton is "very black and very handsome" and magnificently built: "The mahn's a natural prince!" exclaims Ras. "In Africa this mahn be a chief, a black king" (chap. 17). Not for nothing does he figure in the Brotherhood's symbolic poster as a representative of the future, for both in the book and in the poster Clifton is an idealized, emblematic figure. By the end of chapter 20, however, Clifton is dead, shot while resisting arrest in a deliberately self-destructive act.

Clifton's fall from black icon to seller of the obscene Sambo dolls takes place mainly off-stage, but enough indications are given in the text for its course to be sketched. His commitment to the Brotherhood's scientific doctrines is weakened by Ras's anguished plea in chapter 17 that he think black and use his black intelligence. "I suppose," he tells IM, "sometimes a man *has* to plunge outside history . . . otherwise he might kill somebody, go nuts." As we learn in the next chapter, Clifton comes close to doing this in a street fight when he is reported to have beaten up a white Brotherhood member whom it is presumed he had mistaken for a member of a rival group. One may infer that Clifton drops out of the Brotherhood because he realizes what IM grasps only later: that he has been manipulated for its own purposes by the white leadership of the organization. IM discovers the depth of Clifton's self-disgust and despair over the situation of American blacks when he hears the grotesque patter Clifton is using to hawk Sambo dolls in Bryant Park. The dolls are the reductio ad absurdum of the Uncle Tom type, just as Ras in his absurd costume, astride a vegetable-wagon horse and armed with a spear, will become, in the race-riot chapter, the reductio ad absurdum of the black nationalist type.

Clifton does, however, recover a certain degree of dignity in death. His death in chapter 20 is described as happening "like a slow-motion movie" principally to enable the reader to grasp the import of his final moments through the expressive choreography created by the unnaturally slow tempo. Clifton, we may infer, has made a final desperate attempt to recover some dignity through symbolic defiance of white oppression. The result is his death; he becomes "a cooked pigeon," as the cop tells IM. But the last comment made on Clifton in the scene comes from a "round-headed, apple-cheeked boy with thickly-freckled nose and Slavic eyes" and allows the scene to conclude with an endorsement of Clifton's last act. "Even this young epitome of whiteness can recognize the power and dignity in Clifton's final act, and he confers a kind of immortality on him by speaking in the present tense" as he tells IM: "Your friend sure knows how to use his dukes. Biff, bang! One, two and the cop's on his ass!"[74]

After he leaves the site of the shooting, IM wanders down into the subway, his head full of questions about the meaning of Clifton's fall. He is eventually led to a series of realizations that are about as close as *Invisible Man* comes to offering a prescription for effective black leadership. This can be more clearly seen when we recognize that IM's reflections are strongly reminiscent of the third attitude—the positive one—that Ellison had sketched in his *Negro Quarterly* editorial. This was an attitude of "critical participation" in the war effort in particular and white society in general, "based upon a sharp sense of the Negro people's group personality" and upon the belief that "the main task of the Negro people is to work unceasingly towards creating those democratic conditions in which it can live and recreate itself." But for this attitude to prevail, Negro leaders had first to learn "the meaning of the myths and symbols which abound among the Negro masses. For without this knowledge, leadership, no matter how correct its program, will fail. Much in Negro life remains a mystery; perhaps the zoot suit conceals profound political meaning; perhaps the symmetrical frenzy of the Lindy-hop conceals clues to great potential power—if only Negro leaders would solve the riddle." The problem is "psychological" and one of "self-knowledge"—but of the group, not of the individual.[75] Put this way, it would appear that there is a kind of political or group self-knowledge, analogous to, but presumably dependent on, personal self-knowledge (creating the features of the face), that would turn a potential leader into an effective one.

In the subway, IM sees three young men coming along the platform, "tall and slender, walking stiffly with swinging shoulders in their well pressed, too-hot-for-summer suits, their collars high and tight about their necks, their identical hats of black cheap felt set upon the crowns of their heads with a severe formality above their hard conked hair." It was, he says, "as though I'd never seen their like before." The youths seems to be outside of and untouched by the historical time within which the Brotherhood moves; and they seem to suggest a different reading of history—as a gamble rather than a laboratory experiment. And then the sight of black-and-white nuns prompts IM to reflect that in American life the two colors are not equal and that the Brotherhood claim to be above race does not fit the facts of black experience. Finally, IM comes to realize that he has been "asleep, dreaming" during his time in the Brotherhood and that a truer channel for his energies would be to understand and to record black experience.

To record, however, is not to lead. The distinction reminds one that, although IM is a political activist during much of his story, the principal thing we know about his post-chapter 25 life is that he wrote a memoir/novel, *Invisible Man*, which in retrospect may be regarded more as a portrait of the artist as a young man than as a portrait of the black leader in the making. This is why the theme of leadership is not more dominant in *Invisible Man* and why at times it seems a metaphor for creative activity. In any event, after his subway recognitions at the end of chapter 20, and after his realization two chapters later that Brother Jack "doesn't even see me," IM is poised both for a break with the Brotherhood and for the discovery of his invisibility and the possibilities it confers. He is ready, that is, to learn about Rinehart.

8

CHAPTERS 23–25
AND EPILOGUE

O Harlem, Harlem, Harlem . . . a great king held captive in a hall-porter's livery.

Federico García Lorca, "The King of Harlem"

At one point during his argument in chapter 22 with the Brotherhood members over the political effectiveness of Clifton's public funeral, IM insists that what he had done was based on firsthand knowledge of Harlem: "on what I see and feel and on what I've heard, and what I know." What he tells Brother Tobitt shows that he remembers the lesson about history not being a laboratory experiment that he learned in the subway scene at the end of chapter 20: "I've worked among the people up here," IM says. "Ask your [Negro] wife to take you around to the gin mills and the barber shops and the juke joints and the churches, Brother. Yes, and the beauty parlors on Saturdays when they're frying hair. A whole unrecorded history is spoken there, Brother. You wouldn't believe it but it's true." But when IM leaves the meeting and walks over to 125th Street, a series of rapid-fire events causes him to realize how much he himself has not previously noticed, and this leads to the astonishing discovery of a new social and metaphysical reality of Harlem.

Before he can begin to see this reality, however, IM has to put on dark glasses and a wide-brimmed white hat. When he does so, he becomes aware of the existence of a look-alike named Rinehart, who is, after Beckett's Godot, probably the best-known nonappearing character in contemporary literature. Ellison's copious after-the-fact commentary on his novel contains two notable comments on Rinehart, one mainly descriptive, the other wholly interpretative: (1) "Rinehart's role in the formal structure of the narrative is to suggest to the hero a mode of escape from Ras, and a means of applying, in yet another form, his grandfather's cryptic advice to his own situation"; (2) "Rinehart is my name for the personification of chaos. He is also intended to represent America and change. He has lived so long with chaos that he knows how to manipulate it. It is the old theme of [Melville's] *Confidence Man*. He is a figure in a country with no solid past or stable class lines; therefore he is able to move about easily from one to the other."[76] Of the two observations, the first is more helpful because it identifies a key thematic function of Rinehart within the novel: to put to the test the deathbed advice of IM's grandfather. The second observation, however, need not be dismissed as just another interpretative possibility, albeit one that comes from the teller of the tale (whom, according to D. H. Lawrence, one should never trust). As we shall see, these sweeping assertions resemble a kind of interpretative commentary found within the text of *Invisible Man*, especially in its epilogue, where the narrator IM indulges a suspect taste for what Samuel Johnson called the grandeur of generality.

While Beckett's Godot is known through his absence, Rinehart is known through his works. The first person to mistake IM for him—a young woman in a tight-fitting summer dress who reeks of Christmas Night perfume—leaves the reader with the impression that Rinehart is a pimp; while the comments of the two groups of men who mistake IM for Rinehart suggest that he is a stud. In another encounter, IM is mistaken for "Rinehart the number man"; the impression that he is engaged in illegal activities is confirmed by the policeman who demands his accustomed payoff. The one group of men who do not mistake IM's identity tell him that to act like Rinehart "you got to have a smooth tongue, a heartless heart and be ready to do anything." If you are this way, as the next encounter suggests, a lovely exotic-looking girl with ripe breasts may plead with you to come to her bed. The final shape assumed by this protean force is "Rev. B. P. Rinehart, Spiritual Technologist," the handbill for whose storefront church holds out the hope of a more transcendent lift out of the ordinary than even winning the numbers or sexual bliss can provide.

As these encounters succeed each other, IM begins trying "to place Rinehart in the scheme of things. He's been around all the while, but I have been looking in another direction." The questioning thrust of his mind immediately leads on to larger, more speculative questions: "If dark glasses and a white hat could blot out my identity so quickly, who actually was who?" As IM is meditating on these questions in the storefront church, he notices high above him, on the wall, gold letters spelling out the Lord's creative fiat in Genesis, "Let there be light!" a clever adaptation of the comic-strip convention of the just-turned-on light bulb used to signify a sudden realization. What clicks in IM's mind is that Rinehart could be all of his avatars because "his world was possibility and he knew it. He was years ahead of me and I was a fool. . . . The world in which he lived was without boundaries. A vast seething, hot world of fluidity." What this in turn suggests to IM is that the recognition of possibility can lead to liberation of the self: "You could actually make yourself anew." And you could also manipulate your environment to your own advantage, as in the report of the "shoe-shine boy who encountered the best treatment in the South simply by wearing a white turban instead of his usual Dobbs or Stetson."

Such vertiginous speculations seem unreal to IM, just as the comic-strip convention that introduces them seems unrealistic to the reader. Disturbed by "the real chaos" that his thoughts open up, IM hopes that his insights will prove "a brief, emotional illusion." He feels the need to get "the props put back beneath the world," and for that reason takes a cab from Harlem to the affluent West Eighties to see

Hambro, the chief theoretician of the Brotherhood. The visit is followed by the second reflective passage in chapter 23, the extremely important train of thought that develops as IM sits on a bench on Central Park West. Before we examine these two episodes, however, we should first take note of some aspects of Rinehart—and of Rinehartism—that seem sharply to qualify, if not to gainsay, the liberating (if destabilizing) implications of the "let there be light" illumination. When IM goes to the Jolly Dollar bar to test his Rinehart disguise on his friend Maceo, he winds up quarreling with Maceo and is ready to "let him have it as brutally as possible." There is also the wrenching emotion IM feels in the storefront church as he listens to two members of the congregation praise their minister. "They were motherly old women of the southern type and I suddenly felt a nameless despair. I wanted to tell them that Rinehart was a fraud." This same root of piety is touched later in the chapter when IM reflects that it has been quite a day for him, "one that could not have been more shattering even if I had learned that the man whom I'd always called father was actually of no relation to me." The terms of this comparison are extremely interesting, given both the novel's concern with roots, which we have already examined, and the subject of love, which the narrator IM rather abruptly brings up in the epilogue. Whether for good or ill, Rinehartism would seem to involve a severing of roots, of family and regional pieties, as complete as that demanded by the Brotherhood, the very name of which calls attention to its supersession of parental bonds.

During the course of his interview with Hambro, IM discovers another fundamental similarity between the apparently contradictory philosophies of the Brotherhood, with its laboratory experiment, and the gambler Rinehart riding the waves of possibility. The notation at the beginning of the scene is superb.

I was shown into a small, book-lined study by Hambro himself. From another part of the apartment came a child's voice singing *Humpty Dumpty*, awakening humiliating memories of my first

Easter program during which I had stood before the church audience and forgotten the words. . . .

"My kid," Hambro said, "filibustering against going to bed. A real sea lawyer, that kid."

The child was singing *Hickory Dickory Dock*, very fast, as Hambro shut the door. He was saying something about the child and I looked at him with sudden irritation. With Rinehart on my mind, why had I come here?

Hambro's brief comment on his kid's rhetorical inventiveness—a "sea lawyer" is a person who can find a hundred reasons for not doing something—is enough to give this well-to-do white lawyer a distinctive verbal signature and, perhaps, to intimate that his own argument in the ensuing discussion will be comparably specious: *tel arbre, tel fruit*. Like Humpty Dumpty, IM is having a great fall—in his case off the terra firma of the Brotherhood and into chaos. The significance of the humiliating memory of his first Easter program we shall presently see. The very fast singing of "Hickory Dickory Dock" by the overtired child is the perfect musical overture to the scene, suggesting as it does that the scene will recapitulate IM's meeting with the Brotherhood in chapter 22, during which his head begins to whirl "as though I were riding a supersonic merry-go-round." Indeed, his last words to Hambro at the end of this scene contain a telling repetition of this same image: "Everywhere I've turned," he says, "somebody has wanted to sacrifice me for my good—only they were the ones who benefited. And now we start on the old sacrificial merry-go-round. At what point do we stop." And although there is a world of difference between "Hickory Dickory Dock" and the opening of Beethoven's *Fifth Symphony*, which pounds in IM's head at the beginning of chapter 11, the former might be thought to prepare the ground for the moment during their discussion when, as Hambro speaks of "cultivating scientific objectivity" in "a voice that had a smile in it," IM remembers an earlier carousel on which he had been spun. "Suddenly I saw the hospital machine, felt as though locked in again," he says.

The tenor of what Hambro has to tell IM is realpolitik with a vengeance. The Brotherhood, he says, has a larger plan, to which the black Harlem members will have to be sacrificed. Their energies must be curbed because of "scientific necessity." Despite the successful organizational efforts of IM, and despite the moral claim of racial justice, Harlem and its needs cannot "be allowed to upset the tempo of the master plan." At the beginning of their discussion, IM senses some deep change in their relationship. "It was as though my discovery of Rinehart had opened a gulf between us." But as he questions Hambro, IM finds that "somehow I couldn't get the needed urgency into my words, and beneath it all something about Rinehart bothered me, darted just beneath the surface of my mind; something that had to do with me intimately." Though it is never explicitly indicated, this something beneath the surface that bothers IM is surely the felt similarity between Rinehartism and the Brotherhood. We have already noted one such similarity. Another occurs just before IM remembers the hospital scene. "I thought you had learned," Hambro tells him, "that it's impossible *not* to take advantage of the people." "That's Rinehartism—cynicism," replies IM.

Another submerged feeling comes to the surface a little later as IM sits brooding on the park bench. That humiliating memory awakened in him by Hambro's child singing about Humpty Dumpty is the harbinger of a flood of similar remembrances that wash over IM, as he begins to accept an aspect of his past very different from the one symbolized by the yam. He thinks about the "obscene swindle" of the Brotherhood and then about the manifold indignities and humiliations inflicted by them on him and his race. And then, as they rise to the surface of his consciousness, "all past humiliations" are accepted as "precious parts of my experience."

> For the first time . . . I began to accept my past and, as I accepted it, I felt memories welling up within me. . . . Images of past humiliations flickered through my head and I saw that they were more than separate experiences. They were me; they defined me. I was my experiences and my experiences were me . . . and now I looked around a corner of my mind and saw Jack and Norton and Emerson merge into a single white figure. They were very much the same,

each attempting to force his picture of reality upon me and neither giving a hoot in hell for how things looked to me. I was simply a material, a natural resource to be used. I had switched from the arrogant absurdity of Norton and Emerson to that of Jack and the Brotherhood, and it all came out the same.

One way of describing what is happening in this important passage is to say that the subject matter of *Invisible Man* is at last beginning to become the subject matter of the consciousness of IM the character. This of course suggests both that the novel is approaching the narrative present and that when the character IM knows as much about himself as the narrator IM does the narrative will be over. Part of what is left for the character IM to learn has to do with another aspect of the discovery that "I was and yet I was unseen." The awareness of his invisibility brings with it "a kind of morbid fascination" with possibility and with the exploration of different modalities of personality. "My God, what possibilities existed!" His two role models for this exploration are Rinehart and his own grandfather, who at this point IM seems to regard as standing in the same relationship to each other as exemplum to text. Remembering his grandfather, IM decides to overcome the Brotherhood "with yeses, undermine 'em with grins . . . let them swaller you till they vomit or bust wide open." Remembering Rinehart and his lovely girl, he decides he can best obtain inside information about the Brotherhood through using his physical attractiveness to white women. The stage is thus set for the following short chapter, which recounts IM's evening of fun and games with Sybil— an evening interrupted by a telephone call from Harlem bringing news of the race riot.

In chapter 24, *Invisible Man* returns to the subject of black-white sexual relations, and once again dramatizes the degradations and perversions caused by stereotypes and taboos, this time through a detailed rendering of the scene in IM's apartment during which the thoroughly run-of-the-mill and tiresomely tipsy Sybil begs to be raped—to be insulted, stripped, and penetrated, not by an individual, but by a fantasy image of black phallic power. Of course Sybil is not only a woman;

she is also white and as such becomes yet another version of Norton, Emerson, the doctors in the factory hospital, and Jack, all of whom see IM not as an individual but as a black something to be used for their own psychological, political, or sexual purposes. Sybil differs from her predecessors, however, in being incompetent and unsuccessful in her manipulation of IM; it is rather he who is manipulating her, though no more skillfully. Since this is so, the scene between them is a comedy of incompetence that is played for laughs; not without reason does IM wonder at one point if life has "suddenly become a crazy Thurber cartoon."

The first seduction scene in *Invisible Man*—the one in chapter 19 in which IM was bedded by the woman who said she heard tom-toms beating in his voice—was also comic. But there is a telling difference between the two scenes that the reader is surely meant to notice. (It is an example of the variation-in-repetition that signals significance.) In the second case, IM is not successfully manipulated, because through Rinehart he has learned the lesson of invisibility and knows about the freedom of maneuver that comes with the realization that people do not see him as an individual. Indeed, IM has become so well versed in American stereotypes and fantasies that he can flaunt his expertise by inscribing in lipstick on the belly of the unconscious and unpenetrated Sybil the message that she was "raped by Santa Claus." "The image is a perfect one," as Thomas Vogler has said, "for her fantasy of him is no more real than the child's fantasy. She has been taught to believe in the Black sex fantasy as the child is taught to believe in the great magic gift-giver."[77]

One should notice, however, that in IM's playing of the Rinehart role there is little of the cynicism and less of the "heartless heart" that characterize Rinehart's own performances. He rather feels for Sybil "a certain confused pity which I didn't wish to feel," indeed, a pity mixed with "self-disgust." He even begins to reflect on "my *responsibility*" in the matter, a thought totally incompatible with Rinehart-type invisibility. And we should also note the implications of the unpleasant little surprise that is in store for IM on the chapter's closing page.

Chapters 23–25 and Epilogue

A telephone call from "a frantic, unrecognizable voice," who urges IM to get up to Harlem in a hurry, interrupts the fag end of his evening with Sybil. While IM has been acting out his grandfather- and Rinehart-inspired plan to undermine the Brotherhood with yeses by telling them just what they want to hear, the level of tension and of self-destructive violence in Harlem has been rising. What the telephone message intimates turns out to be the case: a full-scale race riot has erupted. Taking with him his briefcase—the one he had been awarded on the night of the battle royal—IM heads for Harlem and for what will be the last, and most pyrotechnical, chapter of his story. But to get over to Harlem from the Hudson River side after getting off the bus from downtown, he has to cross under a bridge. As he begins to do so, he hears "a twitter, a coo, a subdued roar that seemed trying to tell me something, give me some message." When the message from the birds in the girders above arrives, it is found to be excremental. They excrete all over him as he covers his head with his briefcase and runs "the gauntlet, thinking, even the birds; even the pigeons and the sparrows and the goddam gulls." It is a fitting entrance to the riot-torn Harlem stage, on which will occur IM's bitterest and most demoralizing recognitions: that he is still a pawn in the hands of white manipulators; that in assuming the Rinehart disguise he has not outwitted them, but rather played directly into their hands.

Chapter 25 opens con brio with a thunderous noise followed by the appearance of four men pushing a safe, pursued by the police. It is the first of a number of splendid notations of the riot, of which perhaps the two most memorable are the woman who walks past "with a row of about a dozen dressed chickens suspended by their necks from the handle of a new straw broom," and the less practical looter on top of a Borden's milk wagon. "Surrounded by a row of railroad flares, a huge woman in a gingham pinafore sat drinking beer from a barrel which sat before her," shouting out a vendor's blues about Joe Louis and Jim Jeffrey while sloshing the dipper of beer around.

At the beginning of the chapter, IM attaches himself to a group of neighborhood men who first loot a hardware store for the necessary materials and then set fire to the huge and squalid tenement building in which most of them live. What strikes IM most about his brief adventures with this group are the organizational and leadership talents of its leaders, Dupre and Scofield. IM would agree with Keats that though a quarrel in the streets is a thing to be hated, the energies displayed in it are fine. IM is in fact "seized with a fierce sense of exaltation" over this display of black leadership. Dupre is particularly impressive—"a type of man nothing in my life had taught me to see, to understand, or respect, a man outside the scheme till now."

These reflections, however, must be assigned strictly to IM the character, and their constructive implications vis-à-vis black leadership must be seen as sharply qualified by other notations and by the larger context in which their actions take place. Scofield's mindless firing at police with a nickel-plated pistol, for example, does not convey an image of leadership potential. The men's discussion of how the riot started is also telling. A number of accounts of its commencement are offered, but none seems authoritative. IM observes that "somebody has to know." But for Dupre, "Don't nobody know how it started"; and for Scofield, "Hell man, it just exploded." While the two impromptu leaders may be correct in thinking that the efficient cause—the trigger—of the race riot cannot be precisely identified, its formal and final causes are soon to be grasped by IM. Once they are, Dupre and Scofield must shrink in the reader's estimation from the stature of Negro leaders thrown up by the people to that of boys scrambling for loot on an electrified rug.

The truth begins to dawn on IM when he begins to think about the telephone call he has received ("Who wanted me at the district after it was too late?") and then begins to wonder if the general answer to the question of the riot's origin could be that the Brotherhood encouraged it to happen through downgrading their Harlem activities and surrendering their influence to the violent Ras. "Use a nigger to catch a nigger" would be the gist of the Brotherhood's successful manipulation, as a result of which inadequate or absurdly armed blacks (Scofield's nickel-plated pistol, Ras's shield and spear) challenge heavily armed white authority. "It was suicide," reflects IM; "without guns it was suicide. . . . It was not suicide, but murder." IM comes to think that the Brotherhood committee had planned the riot and that he has been as much their tool as he was before he had discovered Rine-hartism and put into practice his grandfather's advice: "A tool just at the very moment I had thought myself free. By pretending to agree I *had* indeed agreed, had made myself responsible."

The extent of IM's blindness, and of the success of his exploiters, is brought home to him when, having fallen through a manhole into a dark underground chamber, he reviews the papers from his briefcase, as he burns them in order to provide illumination—a neat dovetailing of the novel's literal and symbolic levels. His high-school diploma goes first, followed by Clifton's Sambo doll. Then IM pulls from his briefcase, first the anonymous letter he had received at the beginning of chapter 18, which contained the "friendly advice" to go slow in the Brotherhood and remember that "this is a *white man's world,*" and then the slip on which Jack had written his Brotherhood name. He is stunned to discover that the handwriting is the same on each—evidence that bespeaks the enormity of Jack's skills as a manipulator. The specific point is easy to miss. In chapter 18, when IM pondered the question of who could have sent him the letter, there is no reason to doubt his reasoning that its intended effect was to weaken his faith in the Brotherhood "through touching upon my old southern distrust, our fear of white betrayal. It was as though he had learned of my experience with Bledsoe's letters and was trying to use that knowledge to destroy not only me but the whole Brotherhood." One would have thought that at this point in IM's involvement with the Brotherhood Jack would not have wished to introduce a complicating factor. But his prescient masterstroke is to plant the seed of distrust early, presumably in the expectation that it can be made to bear fruit at the desired time. That Jack is correct in his calculations suggests that he knows IM's mind even better than IM himself does. But although his calculations are subtle, the bottom line is brutally simple: his anonymous letter says, in effect, "Keep This Nigger-Boy Running."

What the emptying of the briefcase recapitulates in one way, the repetition of key motifs does in another. The most important of them are the microcosmic-macrocosmic variations of the battle royal in the race-riot chapter, which constitute a richly artistic orchestration of that chapter's closing sentence: "The end was in the beginning." One small example is the nightmarish transmogrification of the naked blond dancer of chapter 1 into "the white, naked, and horribly feminine" mannequins hanging from a lamppost. "'Dummies!' I said aloud. Hairless, bald and sterilely feminine." Any difficulty one might have in hearing this ping is removed when Ras, who had spoken in chapter 17 about what "them stinking [white] women" can do to a black man, throws a spear, piercing one of the hanging dummies.

But the most important first-chapter/last-chapter variation is found in the italicized castration dream at the end of the last chapter, in which other motifs are recapitulated as well. In the dream, the school superintendent from chapter 1 joins Jack, Emerson, Bledsoe, Norton, Ras, and others in pressing around IM, who is lying beside a river of black water, near an armored bridge (the setting obliquely recalls the closing paragraph of chapter 24). Castration is the final stage in the long process of withering into the truth of his psychologically emasculated condition (the factory-hospital chapter is also transmogrified in the dream). Two bloody blobs are severed and cast over the bridge, where they catch on its apex and hang dripping into the water. As the dream ends, the armored bridge, seemingly vivified by the bloody blobs, begins to move off, "striding like a robot, an iron man, whose iron legs clanged doomfully as it moved."

But then IM wakes up, and "in spite of the dream, I was whole," just as in the nightmarish factory-hospital chapter IM remains psychologically whole despite the treatment he receives. Upon reflection, IM decides not to stride off to seek vengeance like an iron man. He will instead adopt a posture more akin to that of the "I" of the dream, who was "full of sorrow and pain." IM will take up residence underground and "try to think things out in peace, or, if not in peace, in quiet."

It was in just this condition of painfully thinking things out that the reader had first encountered the narrator IM over four hundred pages earlier in the prologue to *Invisible Man*. But when IM again addresses the reader directly in the epilogue, which immediately follows chapter 25, we seem in large measure to be listening to a changed man, a less engaged, less anguished, and more philosophical man, who speaks in a more relaxed voice and in remarkably upbeat tones about "the lesson of my own life." One reason for the change is the hindsight made possible by the distance between the climactic event of the narrative of IM the character and the last word of IM the narrator. This distance is virtually the same as that between the prologue and epilogue. But the perspective made possible by this distance seems of itself inadequate to account for the marked differences of mood and statement between the prologue and the twenty-five-chapter narrative on the one hand and the eight-page epilogue on the other. In fact, as we have noted in an earlier chapter, a number of commentators have had serious reservations about the ending, particularly about its positive tone, its stance of being above the black-white battle, its bouncy assertions of love and possibility, and its confident announcement that the hibernation is over and that a decision has been taken to leave the basement room to seek a "socially responsible role" in the outside world.

All these points need to be carefully considered. In doing so it is helpful to cluster Ellison's comments on his novel's epilogue and instructive to note that they are imperfectly compatible with one another. In 1955, the author observed that the epilogue "was necessary to complete the action begun when [IM] set out to write his memoirs." This is a useful reminder of the fact that, given its prologue, the novel would have seemed incomplete without a corresponding epilogue. But that is not to say that there was any necessity for the epilogue to be written in such a different key. Of course, one could take the assertions in the epilogue with a grain of salt and introduce a distinction between the narrator IM and the implied author. Such a distinction is implicit in Ellison's 1963 comment that one shouldn't miss the irony (or assume "that *I* did") of IM speaking of his life as one of "infinite possibilities" while living underground. On the other hand, in a 1972 comment, it is not irony that Ellison stresses, but IM's achievement in writing his story. "After all, that novel is a man's memoir. He gets out of there. The fact that you can read the narrator's memoirs means that he has come out of that hole."[78]

This last point is tricky. Ellison can hardly mean simply that IM has to leave his underground nook in order to get his memoir to a publisher. Perhaps he means that writing a memoir has made IM an author and that this is the socially useful role he was looking for. In any event, the statement Ellison the commentator makes about IM's having come out of "that hole" is, strictly speaking, incorrect. IM does not say in the epilogue or anywhere else that he has come out of hibernation, only that he intends to do so. There is often a big difference between the wish and the deed, and it is easy to understand those who wonder whether IM the narrator (or even Ellison himself) has not confused the two.

The first series of upbeat speculations in the epilogue is found in its long fourth paragraph, which offers what Susan Blake rightly calls a contrived reinterpretation of the grandfather's advice. The rhetorical ruminations ("Could he have meant—hell, he *must* have meant . . . Did he mean to say 'yes' because . . . or did he mean . . . was it that . . . or was it, did he mean that . . . Had he seen . . .") remind one of nothing so much as Ike McCaslin's interminable conversation with his cousin in part 4 of Faulkner's *The Bear,* which similarly chews the indigestible subject of the individual's relationship to his past in the context of the inextricable interrelationship of black and white in the United States. Were IM's cerebrations any more protracted, one might have the same reaction as Crenshaw the attendant does to the crazy vet in chapter 7: "I wish you'd hurry up and git despressive, maybe then you won't talk so damn much." IM's speculations not only move far beyond anything his illiterate grandfather could conceivably have meant; they are also startlingly out of key with virtually everything one has been told or shown about the dynamics of black-white relationships in the preceding four hundred pages of *Invisible Man.* This, plus the fabricated spinning-it-out-of-whole-cloth quality of IM's ruminations, strongly suggests that he is giving voice not to what he believes but what he would like to believe. One might further observe that the passage manifests the unwholesome results of too much thinking, of overworking "the mind, the mind," and that in the context of the entire novel its import relates not to some putative deep meaning in the grandfather's advice, but to the need for IM to find a positive alternative to further thinking. To recall Gerard Manley Hopkins's self-advice: "I do advise / You, jaded, let be; call off thoughts awhile / Elsewhere; leave comfort root-room."

Another bouncy assertion that seems ungrounded in what has gone before is IM's claim that "in spite of all I find that I love." Love is, in Philip Larkin's phrase, a "much-mentioned brilliance," but one place at least where it does not seem to shine and where its name is seldom spoken is in the twenty-five chapters of *Invisible Man*. The two commonest kinds of love in ordinary human experience are familial love and sexual love. *Invisible Man* has little to say or show about either. Concerning the latter, Ellison has said of his novel's protagonist that "such a man as this character would have been incapable of a love affair; it would have been inconsistent with his personality."[79] Even if he were capable, the pickings would have been slim. As commentators on *Invisible Man* have rightly pointed out, the female characters in the novel seem a limited assortment of stereotypes.[80] As for nonsexual love, the only candidate is the folksy Mary Rambo, to whose place IM was hoping to return before his fall into the manhole. Mary, however, is a minor and undeveloped character in the novel (even if we allow ourselves to regard "Out of the Hospital" as part of the text of *Invisible Man*), and love is hardly a word that can be used to describe IM's brief relationship with her.

Mary is of course a maternal figure, but to note this is to prompt one to realize a striking fact about *Invisible Man*: one learns almost nothing about the central character's upbringing or family life. He mentions his father only two or three times in passing; there is one evocative memory of his mother hanging out wash on a windy day; and a single reference in the text informs us that IM has a brother. There are of course prima facie reasons why these relationships do not appear in *Invisible Man*. One is that a dominant subject of the novel is black-white relationships, and this material is so rich and multifaceted that other material cannot be accommodated. Another is that late adolescence and early manhood, the human time frame of the narrative, is a period of mushrooming ego and independent engagement with the outside world, during which parental relationships naturally become recessive.

On the other hand, one might reflect that parents form "the grammar of our emotions," in Brian Moore's phrase, and that in a novel centrally concerned with identity, character formation, and roots, it is peculiar that one learns virtually nothing about the central character's parents or about the first seventeen years of his life. To underline the point, one might call attention to the difference between the account in Ellison's novel of how IM becomes a man and the moving account, in a two-paragraph memoir, of how Ellison himself became a man: by living through his beloved mother's death in a strange city in 1937 when he was twenty-three.[81]

Another possible justification for IM's claim to love is suggested by the sentence in the epilogue following its declaration. "In order to get some of it down I *have* to love." This might be taken to imply that an enabling condition of his being able to tell his tale was the in-the-act-of-writing discovery of positive feelings toward the other characters in his story. This would certainly tally with Ellison's 1974 description, quoted in an earlier chapter, of the moral dimension of the process of novel composition, during which, even in writing about characters who outrage him, the novelist is led to "depict those characters in the breadth of their humanity," to give them the "density of the human," while in doing so a reciprocal process is set in motion through which the novelist is himself humanized.[82] But when one looks back to the novel/memoir that IM the narrator has written, it is no easy matter to find characters so depicted. The sharecropper Jim Trueblood? Yes, and magnificently so. The rabble-rouser Ras? Well yes, but narrowly so. But aside from these two black characters, who? Certainly not Mr. Norton or Bledsoe or Jack or Sybil or any of the other manipulators of IM.

The boldest assertion made in the epilogue is that the world is a place of "infinite possibilities." In the context of the 1950s, there is nothing surprising about such a claim. Irving Howe argued in his 1963 attack on *Invisible Man* that Ellison's "dependence on the post-war *Zeitgeist*" was manifested in "the sudden, unprepared and implausible assertion of unconditioned freedom with which the novel ends." For Howe, "though the unqualified assertion of self-liberation was a favorite strategy among American literary people in the 'fifties, it [was] also vapid and insubstantial. . . . Freedom can be fought for, but it cannot always be willed or asserted into existence. And it hardly seems an accident that even as Ellison's hero asserts the 'infinite possibilities' he makes no attempt to specify them."[83]

Does one have, then, another example of the substitution of the wish for the reality? The answer is not as clear-cut as Howe seems to think. For one thing, unlike the assertion of love, the assertion of possibility in the epilogue is grounded in the body of the novel. "The world is possibility if only you'll discover it," says the vet to IM in chapter 7, shortly before the young man enters Harlem for the first time and senses that it offers him "a new world of possibility." And Rinehart's world is par excellence a world of possibility. We have seen, however, that there were self-deluding limitations to the Rinehart worldview, and it is not surprising that the epilogue confirms an explicit rejection of it: "But what do *I* really want, I've asked myself. Certainly not the freedom of a Rinehart." How then do the "infinite possibilities" celebrated by IM in the epilogue differ from the Rinehart type of possibility?

The key distinction, I believe, is that for IM, the sadder-but-wiser narrator, "infinite possibility" is an internal condition, is in fact a hyperbole for the freedom defined by the old slave woman in the reefer dream of the prologue as "nothing but knowing how to say what I got up in my head." From this point of view, the major significance of IM's story is his ability to tell it—to articulate and to shape into artistic form what weighed so heavily on his mind. With the telling comes a self-understanding and an objectivity exemplified in the fact that for all its demoralizing particulars *Invisible Man* is, formally speaking, more of a comedy than anything else.

In his *Anatomy of Criticism*, Northrop Frye has described the mythos of comedy as emerging out of the winter vision of irony and moving though phases, at the end of which it merges into the summer vision of romance. At its lowest point, the comic vision takes the form of "ironic comedy," which presents a "world in which the comedy consists in inflicting pain on a helpless victim. . . . Ironic comedy brings us to the figure of the scapegoat ritual and the nightmare dream." In the next phase, the comic hero is severely threatened by outside forces and often pushed to a "point of ritual death" before a sudden reversal delivers him from the demonic world. In the succeeding phase, the comic hero may accomplish his own deliverance by escaping from a society that is still too powerful for him. In its later phases, Frye says, the social pressure is less powerful and one sees in sharper relief the informing comic theme of "the integration of society, which usually takes the form of incorporating the central character into it."[84] From our point of view, what is most interesting about Frye's schema is that the end of *Invisible Man* exemplifies this cyclic movement from ironic negation through intervening phases to at least the hope of the reintegration of the central character into society. The castration nightmare at the close of chapter 25 is ironic comedy, while the plunge into the underground hole is the point of ritual death. Taking up life underground is the escape phase, while the epilogue, as we have seen, predicts the imminent end of hibernation and a positive integration with society.

Ralph Ellison has quoted with approbation a statement of Kenneth Burke's about comedy that also throws an important light on the ending of *Invisible Man*: "Comedy should enable us to be observers of ourselves while acting. Its ultimate end would not be passiveness but maximum consciousness. [It should allow] one to 'transcend' himself by noting his own foibles."[85] "Infinite possibilities" may be said to be IM's extravagant phrase for "maximum consciousness," the operation of which is not specified in the epilogue but is instanced in the comic movement of *Invisible Man* toward self-knowledge and the promise of renewal grounded in an awareness of one's mistakes.

From this point of view, the claim concerning "infinite possibilities" can be seen to be grounded in the creative activity of the mind that has produced *Invisible Man*. The beneficial operation of this activity is a subject to which IM returns several times in the epilogue. In its second paragraph he insists that in the preceding narrative "I've tried to articulate exactly what I felt to be the truth." But what he felt to be the truth of his condition at the time he was experiencing it was, of course, not necessarily the truth of his condition. The expressive distortions of the factory-hospital chapter and the castration dream, from both of which IM emerges whole, are the most obvious examples of places in the text where the representation emphasized the subjective response (the felt truth) and not what actually happened. But the result of the artistic representation of personal experience through the creative activity of the mind is self-discovery, and part of what we discover is that what we felt to be the truth is not the whole truth. "The fact is," IM observes, "that you carry part of your sickness within you, at least I do as an invisible man. I carried my sickness and though for a long time I tried to place it in the outside world, the attempt to write it down shows me that at least half of it lay within me."

That is to say, the analysis of the black plight contained in the Louis Armstrong recording of "Black and Blue" has been found to have only a partial applicability to the condition of IM, who, by the epilogue, has realized that his "sin" is not only "in my skin" but also within himself. IM further observes that the attempt to express his anger through telling his story, "the very act of trying to put it all down," has "negated some of the anger and some of the bitterness." The after-the-fact discovery of his own involvement in his misfortunes is indicated by his use of comic motifs in representing his earlier history, just as the expressive nodes are used to represent the anguish that IM the character felt at certain points in the past. The most obvious example is IM's presentation of his earlier self as that comic staple, the naif, who has painfully to learn the way things are through a series of stumbling misadventures and comic predicaments—rug pulls and boomerangs—in which much of the comedy is at his own expense, and in which his most farcically comic humiliation—being bespattered by the birds—echoes the comic humiliation of the Bledsoe surrogate in chapter 12, who has a "full and foul" spittoon emptied on his head. (Jack's comic humiliation takes a different form: from the point of view of the comic motifs in *Invisible Man,* the eruption of his glass eye becomes a neat bit of farcical leveling.)

But comic motifs and liberating humor are only two of the strands in the complex design of the tapestry IM fashions while living in his basement room. And while the creative activity of the mind has brought him to realize his complicity in his own misfortunes and has negated some of his anger and bitterness, he is, he says, still confused and still wounded. Though he admits that he is "implicated [in] and partially responsible" for his condition, he has been badly hurt by his experiences, "hurt to the point of abysmal pain, hurt to the point of invisibility." That is to say, invisibility is a symptom of his affliction, not part of the cure. The latter comes, if at all, with "having tried to put it down." The effect of this attempt may be said to resemble that of the hoped-for result of the therapy offered in the brightly lit basement room of the Lafargue Psychiatric Clinic in Harlem, as described by Ralph Ellison in an article written in 1948, in the middle of the composition of *Invisible Man.* "The phrase 'I'm nowhere'," Ellison wrote, "expresses the feeling borne in on many Negroes that they have no stable recognized place in society. One's identity drifts in a capricious reality in which even the most commonly held assumptions are questionable. One 'is' literally, but one is nowhere; one wanders dazed in a ghetto maze, a 'displaced person' of American democracy." The "modest achievement" sought by the staff of the clinic was "to give each bewildered patient an insight into the relation between his problems and his environment, and out of this understanding to reforge the will to endure in a hostile world."[86]

Insight into his condition and the will to endure: these, I would say, the epilogue shows IM to have achieved. They add up to a distinctly more qualified and somber state of mind than that which IM claims for himself at times during the epilogue. But, after all, IM always was prone to exaggeration—both the narrating self in his techniques of representation and the experiencing self in his I-yam-what-I-am-type gestures and his repeated accentuations of the positive. As for the questions of what specifically IM will do when he leaves his basement room, what particular form his endurance in a hostile world will take, and what socially responsible role he will play: these are quite properly left unanswered by the ending of *Invisible Man*, which concludes with its central character and narrator on the threshold of another story.

In the last sentence of *Invisible Man*, IM raises a final possibility. He addresses the reader directly and suggests that, having read his story, the reader has perhaps reached a new threshold of awareness, just as IM has as a result of having written it: "Who knows but that, on the lower frequencies, I speak for you?" At the end of *Notes from Underground*, Dostoyevski's alienated narrator had made a similar point in addressing his reader directly and suggesting that "we" actually had a great deal in common and that in his own life he had simply carried to an extreme what "you" the reader has not dared carry halfway. But despite this and other similarities, there is one fundamental difference between the endings of the autobiographical accounts of the two underground men. Dostoyevski's novella has a closed ending; it is abundantly clear by its conclusion that the narrator has had the opportunity to change, has failed or been unable to do so, and will never be any different from what he now is—will never leave the psychological underground in which he has immured himself. *Invisible Man*, on the other hand, has an open ending; as such it resembles *Notes from Underground* less than it does American novels like *Huckleberry Finn* that conclude on a note of possibility. Of course the degree of possibility held open at the end of *Invisible Man* is hardly that of Mark Twain's novel, the first-person narrator of which closes his story by saying that he is opting out of the only society he knows and intends to "light out for the Territory ahead of the rest." There is no new territory for which to light out at the end of *Invisible Man*, which concludes with IM on the brink of opting *into* the only society he has ever known—a society in which, despite all that has happened to him, he believes he may have a constructive role to play.

NOTES

1. *Going to the Territory* (New York: Random House, 1986), 250, 254, 255, 257, 239, 242, 244.

2. *Shadow and Act* (New York: Random House, 1964), 25–26, 307–8.

3. *Shadow and Act,* 80.

4. *Shadow and Act,* 298, 296, 297.

5. "Recent Negro Fiction," *New Masses* 40 (August 1941): 22; *Shadow and Act,* 94.

6. *Shadow and Act,* 140; "Study and Experience: An Interview with Ralph Ellison," *Massachusetts Review* 18 (1977): 418; *Shadow and Act,* 120.

7. *Shadow and Act,* 171.

8. *Shadow and Act,* 39.

9. *Shadow and Act,* 189.

10. Albert Murray, *The Omni-Americans: New Perspectives on Black Experience and American Culture* (New York: Outerbridge & Dienstfrey, 1970), 167.

11. *Shadow and Act,* 78–79.

12. *Going to the Territory,* 289.

13. Joseph Frank, "Ralph Ellison and a Literary 'Ancestor': Dostoevsky," *New Criterion* (September 1983): 12.

14. "'A Completion of Personality': A Talk with Ralph Ellison," in *Ralph Ellison: A Collection of Critical Essays*, ed. John Hersey (Englewood Cliffs, N.J.: Prentice-Hall, 1974), 14.

15. *Shadow and Act*, 141.

16. "The Visible Man," *Newsweek* (12 August 1963): 82.

17. "An Interview with Ralph Ellison," *Tamarack Review* 32 (1964): 20; *Going to the Territory*, 273.

18. "The Natural History of German Life," in *Essays of George Eliot*, ed. Thomas Pinney (New York: Columbia University Press, 1963), 270–71.

19. D. H. Lawrence, *Studies in Classic American Literature* (Garden City, N.Y.: Doubleday Anchor, 1951), 13.

20. Philip Roth, *Reading Myself and Others* (New York: Farrar, Straus, 1975), 128, 120, 135.

21. Both reviews are quoted in Larry Neal, "Ellison's Zoot Suit," *Black World* 20 (1970); reprinted in Hersey, *Ralph Ellison; Essays*, 62–63.

22. Saul Bellow, review in *Commentary* 13 (June 1952): 608; William Barrett, review in *American Mercury* 74 (June 1952): 100–101, 103.

23. Irving Howe, *Celebrations and Attacks* (New York: Horizon, 1979), 29–31.

24. Richard Chase, review in *Kenyon Review* 14 (1952): 679, 682; Delmore Schwartz, review in *Partisan Review* 19 (1952): 359.

25. Carol and Richard Ohmann have called attention to a similar tendency in reviewers and critics of an American novel published the year before *Invisible Man*; see their "Reviews, Critics, and *The Catcher in the Rye*," *Critical Inquiry* 3 (1976): 15–37.

26. Robert Bone, *The Negro Novel in America* (New Haven: Yale University Press, 1965), 152, 212, 246.

27. Addison Gayle, Jr., *The Black Aesthetic* (Garden City, N.Y.: Doubleday Anchor, 1972), 392; *The Way of the New World: The Black Novel in America* (Garden City, N.Y.: Doubleday Anchor, 1976), xxii, xxiii, 257.

28. Irving Howe, *A World More Attractive* (New York: Horizon, 1963), 100, 112, 114.

29. "Study and Experience," 424.

30. Hersey, ed., *Ralph Ellison: Essays*, 18.

31. "Study and Experience," 426.

32. George E. Kent, "Ralph Ellison and Afro-American Folk and Cultural Tradition," *CLA Journal* 13 (1970); reprinted in Hersey, ed., *Ralph Ellison: Essays*, 169.

33. John Bayley, *The Uses of Division: Unity and Disharmony in Literature* (London: Chatto & Windus, 1976), 11.

Notes

34. Houston A. Baker, Jr., "To Move without Moving: An Analysis of Creativity and Commerce in the Trueblood Episode," *PMLA* 98 (1983): 843–44.

35. Susan L. Blake, "Ritual and Rationalization: Black Folklore in the Works of Ralph Ellison," *PMLA* 94 (1979): 122–23, 134, 126, 130.

36. G. K. Chesterton, *Appreciations and Criticisms of the Works of Charles Dickens* (Port Washington, N.Y.: Kennikat Press, 1966), 52.

37. *Going to the Territory,* 242.

38. *Going to the Territory,* 60–61.

39. *Shadow and Act,* 178.

40. "Author's Note" to "Out of the Hospital and under the Bar," in *Soon, One Morning: New Writing by American Negroes 1940–1962,* ed. Herbert Hill (New York: Knopf, 1963), 243.

41. Marcus Klein, *After Alienation: American Novels of Midcentury* (Cleveland: World, 1962), 144; Robert G. O'Meally, *The Craft of Ralph Ellison* (Cambridge: Harvard University Press, 1980), 85.

42. "Interview with Ralph Ellison," 17.

43. O'Meally, *The Craft of Ralph Ellison,* 12–13, 196; "Ralph Ellison," in *American Writers: A Collection of Literary Biographies* (supplement 2, part 1), ed. A. Walton Litz (New York: Scribner's, 1981), 224.

44. *Going to the Territory,* 57; *Shadow and Act,* 174.

45. Hersey, *Ralph Ellison: Essays,* 12.

46. *Shadow and Act,* 56.

47. See Leon Forrest, "Luminosity from the Lower Frequencies," *Carleton Miscellany* 18 (1980): 91.

48. Henry David Thoreau, *Walden,* ed. J. Lyndon Shanley (Princeton: Princeton University Press, 1971), 76.

49. Ibid., 77.

50. Sigmund Freud, *Civilization and Its Discontents,* ed. and trans. James Strachey (New York: Norton, 1962), 51.

51. Baker, "To Move without Moving," 831.

52. Frank, "Ancestor," 16.

53. Freud, *Civilization and Its Discontents,* 51.

54. "American Humor," appendix to Elwyn Ellison Breux, "Comic Elements in Selected Prose Works by James Baldwin, Ralph Ellison, and Langston Hughes" (Diss. Oklahoma State University, 1971), 157, 148, 153, 155.

55. Quoted in Russell G. Fischer, "*Invisible Man* as History," *CLA Journal* 17 (1974): 343.

56. See O'Meally, *The Craft of Ralph Ellison*, 12–25; and Robert J. Norrell, *Reaping the Whirlwind: The Civil Rights Movement in Tuskegee* (New York: Random House, 1985), 19–30.

57. *The American Negro Reference Book*, ed. John P. Davis (Englewood Cliffs, N.J.: Prentice-Hall, 1966), 119.

58. Leslie Fiedler, *An End to Innocence: Essays on Culture and Politics* (Boston: Beacon Press, 1955), 142–51.

59. Sigmund Freud, *Totem and Taboo*, trans. James Strachey (London: Routledge & Kegan Paul, 1950), 145.

60. Jonathan Baumbach, "Nightmare of a Native Son: Ralph Ellison's *Invisible Man*," *Critique* 6 (1963): 53.

61. *Shadow and Act*, 231.

62. *American Institutions and Their Influence* (New York: Barnes, 1851), 338; quoted in Fischer, "*Invisible Man* as History," 355.

63. *Soon, One Morning*, ed. Herbert Hill, 244–90.

64. *Soon, One Morning*, ed. Herbert Hill, 243; "Study and Experience," 429.

65. *Soon, One Morning*, ed. Herbert Hill, 243.

66. *Shadow and Act*, 178–79.

67. Bellow, review in *Commentary*, 609.

68. Klein, *After Alienation*, 108, 118.

69. Baker, "To Move without Moving," 832.

70. *Going to the Territory*, 61–62.

71. *Shadow and Act*, 86.

72. *Going to the Territory*, 44–45.

73. "Editorial Comment," *Negro Quarterly* 1 (1943): 295–97.

74. Stephen B. Bennett and William W. Nichols, "Violence in Afro-American Fiction: An Hypothesis," *Modern Fiction Studies* 17 (1971); reprinted in Hersey, *Ralph Ellison: Essays*, 173.

75. "Editorial Comment," 298, 301–2.

76. *Shadow and Act*, 56–57, 181–82.

77. Thomas A. Vogler, "*Invisible Man*: Somebody's Protest Novel," *Iowa Review* 1 (1970); reprinted in *The Merrill Studies of "Invisible Man*," ed. Ronald Gottesman (Columbus, Ohio: Merrill, 1971), 63.

78. *Shadow and Act*, 179, 109; "Ralph Ellison," *Interviews with Black Writers*, ed. John O'Brien (New York: Liveright, 1973), 73.

79. *Shadow and Act*, 180.

80. See Carolyn W. Sylvander, "Ralph Ellison's *Invisible Man* and Female Stereotypes," *Negro American Literature Forum* 9 (1975): 77–79.

Notes

81. "February," *Saturday Review* (1 January 1955): 25.

82. Hersey, *Ralph Ellison: Essays*, 18.

83. Howe, *A World More Attractive*, 115.

84. Northrop Frye, *Anatomy of Criticism* (Princeton: Princeton University Press, 1957), 45, 179–80.

85. *Going to the Territory*, 184.

86. *Shadow and Act*, 300, 302.

SELECTED BIBLIOGRAPHY

Primary Works

(a) Books

Invisible Man. New York: Random House, 1952. Special thirtieth anniversary edition, with an introduction by the author, published in 1982.

Shadow and Act. New York: Random House, 1964. A collection of essays, interviews, reviews.

Going to the Territory. New York: Random House, 1986. Second collection of essays, lectures, and interviews.

(b) Uncollected short fiction, articles, and interviews.

"Flying Home." In *Cross Section*, edited by Edwin Seaver, 469–85. New York: Fischer, 1944. Reprinted in *Dark Symphony: Negro Literature in America*, edited by James A. Emanuel and Theodore L. Gross, 254–70. New York: Free Press, 1968. Story.

"King of the Bingo Game." *Tomorrow* 4 (November 1944): 29–33. Reprinted in *Dark Symphony*, 271–79. Story.

"Talk with Ralph Ellison." Conducted by Harvey Breit. *New York Times Book Review* (4 May 1952): 26–27.

"Sidelights on Invisibility." Interview with Rochelle Girson. *Saturday Review* (14 March 1953): 20, 49.

"Out of the Hospital and under the Bar." In *Soon, One Morning: New Writing*

Selected Bibliography

by *American Negroes, 1940–1962,* edited by Herbert Hill, 242–90. New York: Knopf, 1963. Originally part of the manuscript of *Invisible Man,* this narrative chunk describes how, through the help of Mary Rambo, the narrator escapes from the factory hospital and reaches Harlem.

"An Interview with Ralph Ellison." Conducted by Allen Geller. *Tamarack Review* 32 (1964), 3–24. Reprinted in *The Black American Writer—Volume I: Fiction,* edited by C. W. E. Bigsby, 153–68. Deland, Florida: Everett/Edwards, 1969.

"'A Completion of Personality': A Talk with Ralph Ellison." In *Ralph Ellison: A Collection of Critical Essays,* edited by John Hersey, 1–19. Englewood Cliffs, N.J.: Prentice-Hall, 1974.

"Study and Experience: An Interview with Ralph Ellison." *Massachusetts Review* 18 (1977): 417–35.

Secondary Works

(a) Books

O'Meally, Robert G. *The Craft of Ralph Ellison.* Cambridge: Harvard University Press, 1980. Biographical-critical study.

(b) Collections

CLA [College Language Association] Journal (special Ralph Ellison issue), 13, 3 (March 1970).

Gottesman, Ronald, ed. *The Merrill Studies in "Invisible Man."* Columbus, Ohio: Merrill, 1971.

Harper, Michael S. and John Wright, eds. *The Carleton Miscellany* (special issue: A Ralph Ellison Festival), 18, 3 (Winter 1980).

Hersey, John, ed. *Ralph Ellison: A Collection of Critical Essays.* Twentieth-Century Views. Englewood Cliffs, N.J.: Prentice-Hall, 1974.

Reilly, John M., ed. *Twentieth Century Interpretations of "Invisible Man": A Collection of Critical Essays.* Englewood Cliffs, N.J.: Prentice-Hall, 1970.

Trimmer, Joseph F., ed. *A Casebook on Ralph Ellison's "Invisible Man."* New York: Crowell, 1972.

(c) General studies containing discussion of *Invisible Man.*

Bone, Robert. *The Negro Novel in America.* New Haven: Yale University Press, 1958; rev. 1965.

Byerman, Keith E. *Fingering the Jagged Grain: Tradition and Form in Recent Black Fiction*. Athens: University of Georgia Press, 1985.

Cooke, Michael G. *Afro-American Literature in the Twentieth Century: The Achievement of Intimacy*. New Haven: Yale University Press, 1984.

Kazin, Alfred. *Bright Book of Life: American Novelists and Storytellers from Hemingway to Mailer*. Boston: Little, Brown, 1973.

Klein, Marcus. *After Alienation: American Novels in Midcentury*. Cleveland: World, 1962.

Rosenblatt, Roger. *Black Fiction*. Cambridge: Harvard University Press, 1974.

Stepto, Robert B. *From Behind the Veil: A Study of Afro-American Narrative*. Urbana: University of Illinois Press, 1979.

Tanner, Tony. *City of Words: American Fiction 1950–1970*. London: Cape, 1971.

(d) Articles

Abrams, Robert E. "The Ambiguities of Dreaming in Ellison's *Invisible Man*." *American Literature* 49 (1978): 592–603.

Baker, Houston A., Jr. "A Forgotten Prototype: *The Autobiography of an Ex-Colored Man* and *Invisible Man*." In his *Singers of Daybreak: Studies in Black American Literature*, 17–31. Washington, D.C.: Howard University Press, 1974.

———. "To Move without Moving: An Analysis of Creativity and Commerce in Ralph Ellison's Trueblood Episode." *PMLA* 98 (1983): 828–45. Reprinted in Baker's *Blues, Ideology, and Afro-American Literature: A Vernacular Theory*. Chicago: University of Chicago Press, 1984; and in *Black Literature and Literary Theory*, edited by Henry Louis Gates, Jr. New York: Methuen, 1984. Important revisionary reading.

Blake, Susan L. "Ritual and Rationalization: Black Folklore in the Works of Ralph Ellison." *PMLA* 94 (1979): 121–36. Important revisionary reading.

Bluestein, Gene. "The Blues as a Literary Theme." In his *Black and White in American Culture: An Anthology from "The Massachusetts Review,"* edited by Jules Chametzky and Sidney Kaplan, 229–55. [Amherst:] University of Massachusetts Press, 1969.

Fischer, Russell G. "*Invisible Man* as History." *CLA Journal* 17 (1974): 338–67. On the novel's sociohistorical dimension.

Forrest, Leon. "Luminosity from the Lower Frequencies." *Carleton Miscellany* 18 (1980): 82–97.

Frank, Joseph. "Ralph Ellison and a Literary 'Ancestor': Dostoevsky." *New Criterion* 11 (1983): 11–21.

Selected Bibliography

Goede, William. "On Lower Frequencies: The Buried Men in Wright and Ellison." *Modern Fiction Studies* 15 (1969): 483–501.

Kent, George. "Ralph Ellison and Afro-American Folk and Cultural Tradition." *CLA Journal* 13 (1970): 265–76. Reprinted in his *Blackness and the Adventure of Western Culture*. Chicago: Third World Press, 1972; and in Hersey.

Kostelanetz, Richard. "The Politics of Ellison's Booker: *Invisible Man* as Symbolic History." *Chicago Review* 19 (1967): 5–26. Reprinted in Trimmer. On the novel's sociohistorical dimension.

Neal, Larry. "Ellison's Zoot Suit." *Black World* 20 (1970), 31–50. Reprinted in Hersey.

Skerrett, Joseph T. "The Wright Interpretation: Ralph Ellison and the Anxiety of Influence." *Massachusetts Review* 21 (1980): 196–212.

Vogler, Thomas A. "*Invisible Man:* Somebody's Protest Novel." *Iowa Review* 1 (1970): 64–82. Reprinted in Gottesman and in Hersey.

Wright, John. "Dedicated Dreamer, Consecrated Acts: Shadowing Ellison." *Carleton Miscellany* 18 (1980): 142–98. Excellent discussion of Ellison's intellectual development.

Biographical and Bibliographical Studies

Covo, Jacqueline. *The Blinking Eye: Ralph Ellison and His American, French, German, and Italian Critics, 1952–1971.* Metuchen, New Jersey: Scarecrow Press, 1974.

Giza, Joanne. "Ralph Ellison." In *Black American Writers: Bibliographical Essays*, vol. 2, edited by M. Thomas Inge et al., 47–71. New York: St. Martin's, 1978.

O'Meally, Robert. "Ralph Ellison." In *American Writers: A Collection of Literary Biographies* (supplement 2, part 1, W. H. Auden to O. Henry), edited by A. Walton Litz, 221–52. New York: Scribner's, 1981.

INDEX

Index

101–3; "Harlem is Nowhere," 4–5; "Out of the Hospital and Under the Bar," 78–81, 119; "Society, Morality, and the Novel," 2; "Twentieth-Century Fiction and the Black Mask of Humanity," 2–3; "The World and the Jug," 20
Emerson, Ralph Waldo, 69

Faulkner, William, 3, 9, 61; *Absalom, Absalom!*, 53; *The Bear*, 118
Fiedler, Leslie: "Come Back to the Raft Ag'in, Huck Honey!" 70
Fitzgerald, F. Scott: *The Great Gatsby*, 27
Frank, Joseph, 8, 53
Freud, Sigmund: *Civilization and its Discontents*, 49, 57; *Totem and Taboo*, 70
Frye, Northrop: *Anatomy of Criticism*, 121–22

Garvey, Marcus, 4, 92
Gayle, Addison, Jr., 18–19; *Black Aesthetic*, 18–19; *The Way of the New World: The Black Novel in America*, 19

Hawthorne, Nathaniel, 2; *The Blithedale Romance*, 27–28
Hemingway, Ernest, 1, 3, 8
Hersey, John, 20
Hopkins, Gerard Manley, 119
Howe, Irving, 17, 121; "Black Boys and Native Sons," 19
Hurston, Zora Neale: *Their Eyes Were Watching God*, 5

James, Henry, 1, 2
Johnson, James Weldon: *Autobiography of an Ex-Colored Man*, 5

Johnson, Lonnie: "She's My Mary," 95
Johnson, Samuel, 106
Joyce, James, 8; *Portrait of the Artist as a Young Man*, 100; *Ulysses*, 8, 12–13

Keats, John, 114
Killens, John, 15–16
Klein, Marcus, 37, 85

Larkin, Philip, 119
Lawrence, D. H., 13, 106
Lorca, Federico García: "The King of Harlem," 105

Malcolm X: *Autobiography*, 5
Malraux, André, 8
Melville, Herman, 2, 19; *The Confidence Man*, 106; *Moby-Dick*, 27–28
Moore, Brian, 120
Moton, Robert Russa, 59

O'Meally, Robert, 37; *The Craft of Ralph Ellison*, 40

Park, Robert and Burgess, Ernest: *Introduction to the Science of Sociology*, 3

Raglan, Lord: *The Hero*, 97
Roth, Philip: "Writing American Fiction," 13–14

Salinger, J. D.: *The Catcher in the Rye*, 27
Schwartz, Delmore, 18
Smith, Bessie: "Backwater Blues," 31
Smith, Trixie: "Trixie's Blues," 84
Steinbeck, John, 3

Thoreau, Henry David: *Walden*, 47
Tocqueville, Alexis de, 75

Toomer, Jean: *Cane*, 5
Twain, Mark, 2, 9; *Huckleberry
    Finn*, 70, 71, 125

Vogler, Thomas, 112

Washington, Booker T., 4, 37, 39,
    58, 74; *Up from Slavery*, 5

Whitman, Walt: *Leaves of Grass*, 71
Wright, Richard, 5–6, 16, 19; *Black
    Boy*, 5: *The Man Who Lived
    Underground*, 5; *Native Son*, 5,
    16, 19

ABOUT THE AUTHOR

Kerry McSweeney is Molson Professor of English at McGill University in Montréal, where he teaches nineteenth-century British and American literature. He is the author of *Tennyson and Swinburne as Romantic Naturalists* (1981), *Four Contemporary Novelists: Angus Wilson, Brian Moore, John Fowles, V. S. Naipaul* (1983), *"Middlemarch"* (1984), and *"Moby-Dick": Ishmael's Mighty Book* (1986). He has edited *Diversity and Depth in Fiction: Selected Critical Writings of Angus Wilson* (1983) and coedited Carlyle's *Sartor Resartus* (1987). In addition, he has written a monograph on Mordecai Richler and many articles and review essays. From 1972 to 1980 he was the editor of *Queen's Quarterly: A Canadian Review.*